A
Lifelong Quest
for Peace

Daisaku Ikeda welcoming Dr. Linus Pauling, the "Father of Modern Chemistry" (Soka University Los Angeles campus)

A
Lifelong Quest for Peace

A *Dialogue*
Linus Pauling   Daisaku Ikeda

Translated and Edited by
Richard L. Gage

Jones and Bartlett Publishers
Boston   London

Editorial, Sales, and Customer Service Offices

Jones and Bartlett Publishers
One Exeter Plaza
Boston, MA 02116

Jones and Bartlett Publishers International
PO Box 1498
London W6 7RS
England

Library of Congress Cataloging-in-Publication Data

Pauling, Linus, 1901–
    A lifelong quest for peace: a dialogue between Linus Pauling and Daisaku
Ikeda/translated and edited by Richard L. Gage.
        p.   cm.
    Includes index.
    ISBN 0-86720-278-5 ISBN 0-86720-277-7 (pbk.)
    1. Peace.   I. Ikeda, Daisaku.   II. Gage, Richard L.
JX1963.P3257   1992
327.172—dc20   92-14170
                                                                CIP

Printed in the United States of America
96 95 94 93 92   10 9 8 7 6 5 4 3 2 1

Contents

Contents

Preface

Much of the vast sums spent by the nations of the world on military establishments is pure waste. By its very nature war today threatens to involve nuclear weapons. And a full-scale nuclear war would almost certainly mean the end of civilization and possibly the end of the human race. Entertaining the mere possibility of such a conflict is completely irrational.

The destruction caused by World War I and World War II was so great that neither the winners nor the losers benefited. All nations suffered severely in terms both of lives lost and material wealth destroyed. A third world war would be different: it would wreak irreparable damage not only on the warring nations, but on everyone else on Earth as well.

The time has come to recognize these facts and to take the actions they indicate. We must save the money now being wasted on militarism and use it to benefit human beings everywhere.

For decades, both Daisaku Ikeda and I have been working to achieve the goals of disarmament, world understanding, and universal peace. We discussed these problems and the future of humankind at a meeting we held at Soka University, Los Angeles, in 1987; and our efforts to deal with the current crisis are described in detail in the dialogue contained in the following pages.

I hope as many people as possible will read our dialogue and then decide for themselves how they personally can serve the purpose of achieving the goal of eliminating war and building a peaceful world.

Linus Pauling

Preface

The rain had just lifted, leaving the vaulted California sky transparently blue over a grove of eucalyptus trees rustling in the breeze. Doctor Linus Pauling had been kind enough to fly to Los Angeles from San Francisco to join me in conducting a dialogue on the campus of the Soka University Los Angeles branch, which was just about to initiate its teaching mission at this time.

One of the greatest scientists of the twentieth century, Dr. Pauling is an unostentatious, modest, and tolerant person. Although this was our first meeting, I felt as if I had already known him for a long time. I vividly remember how he said, smiling, "I'm happy to cooperate in any way that I can for the sake of world peace."

Our discussion covered a wide range of topics, including science, peace, and his own warm recollections of such figures as Albert Einstein. Before we knew it, the allotted amount of time had flown by. Realizing we could not possibly say all that needed saying at one meeting, we decided to continue our exchange in written form.

In spite of a busy schedule involving research in chemistry and medicine and writing, Dr. Pauling enthusiastically devoted as much time as he could to completing our task, working mostly at his house on the California coast at Big Sur.

His contributions to the dialogue reveal much about a man who, in addition to being justly known as the father of modern chemistry, has made revolutionary achievements in biology and medicine as well. The only person ever to have been awarded two unshared Nobel Prizes (1954 for chemistry and 1962 for peace), he truly deserves to stand with Galileo, Newton, Darwin, Curie, and Einstein as one of the greatest scientists of history.

Born in 1901, Linus Pauling has experienced two world wars and, throughout an age threatened by nuclear conflict, has consistently advocated peace and promoted opposition to the use of military force. Even in the face of sometimes harsh criticism, he has never abandoned his faith in true humanism and justice.

Since it relates in direct and clear form memories of his childhood, his development as a scientist, his beliefs as a pacifist, and many episodes about his life and the people he has known, I am certain this dialogue will give a large number of people an opportunity to know Dr. Pauling better. Both he and I will be overjoyed if the book provides hints that can help young people solve the problems of the century to come. Indeed, the desire to do precisely that was the starting point of the whole dialogue project.

Daisaku Ikeda

Foreword

Linus Pauling is one of the greatest scientists of our 20th century. Whether he is the most outstanding chemist may be debated, but there is little doubt that the breadth of his scientific knowledge and the extent of his contributions to the gamut of sciences from physics to chemistry to biology and to the social sciences are unmatched. Surely then, a conversation with him that covers the whole range of his attitudes and feelings about science and human affairs is a welcome opportunity to meet and become better acquainted.

Daisaku Ikeda, an eminent humanist and philosopher, is the experienced interlocutor who has engaged in a number of perceptive and provocative dialogues with world leaders. In this instance, an individual steeped in the Buddhist tradition and raised in a traditional Far Eastern culture, queries a rational scientist born and bred in the relatively wild American Far West. What was his family setting? How did he enter science? Where did he get his novel ideas? What were his ties to family and society? Does he believe in God?

The average person will recognize the name Linus Pauling and might associate it with a Nobel Prize in science, a second Nobel Prize for peace, or even with the benefits of megadoses of Vitamin C. These are the themes that are featured in Pauling's responses to Ikeda's reflections and questions. What emerges and might not be widely known about Pauling is his courage and vision in probing the molecular basis of complex biologic phenomena. Even as a young chemist, he was fascinated by immunity, anesthesia, and the pathologic chemistry of disease. His systematic study of proteins, particularly antibodies and hemoglobin gave us novel insights into protein structure and elucidated the nature of sickle-cell anemia. For these achievements he richly deserved a third Nobel award in medicine.

Despite popular attention to science, the nature of scientific discovery remains a mystery to lay people. Few realize how close to art is the imagination and creativity that advances science. It might seem, especially in the computer age, that exploration into the scientific unknown can be programmed and systemized. Not so. Whereas advanced techniques furnish a wealth of information at the push of buttons, the buttons to be pushed and in what order and how to distinguish meaningful data from background noise remain an artistic enterprise and is driven by the urge to understand nature.

Where the exercise of imagination in science differs from that in fine arts, law, business, or religion, is in the rigid discipline that demands objectivity, preferably expressed in numerical values, and verifiable by others. In contrast to the rules of law, scientists stand guilty in their claims until proven innocent by the burden of evidence and corroboration by others. In this regard, Pauling differs from most. From his vast command of scientific disciplines and high intelligence, he intuits conceptions which he regards as true until proven false. He stands innocent until proven guilty. To his everlasting credit, he has been right often enough to excuse this unorthodox attitude.

Pauling's conviction that humans benefit from doses of vitamin C, as much as 100 times greater than the recommended intake, is a recent example of his unusual approach. It has touched a raw nerve among physicians and nutritionists. His evangelism for these huge amounts to control a variety of ailments from the common cold to cancer has been highly controversial and is one of many instances of our pathetic ignorance of human nutrition. Of course, Pauling has never shrunk back from controversy. He offers theoretical, anecdotal, and some experimental evidence to support his position. While his argument that certain individuals with an inborn metabolic error or disease might profit from megadoses of this highly reactive molecule, it can be imagined that others not so affected might react adversely.

Pauling's vigorous campaigning for peace, disarmament, and civil rights have also earned him disapprobation, at times from his country, university, and colleagues. He weathered these storms and emerged victorious in the battle to stop the atmospheric testing of atomic bombs. His oratorical skills, indefatigable persistence and uncanny talent to focus media attention on this issue earned him the Nobel Prize for which he professes the most pride.

Foreword

Now hear it from Linus Pauling at 91—lively, sharp and energetic, as involved as ever in issues of human welfare and civil rights, still doing science, and published regularly.

Arthur Kornberg
Professor of Biochemistry
Stanford University
Stanford, California
January 2, 1992.

Dr. Linus Pauling and Daisaku Ikeda

A
Lifelong Quest
for Peace

1

Satisfaction in Living

Recollections

Ikeda: Doctor Pauling, the wealth of experience you have amassed during your long and distinguished life amounts to a treasure trove of invaluable suggestions. In the course of this dialogue, I hope to delve into those fields in which you have been especially prominent—science, medicine, and peace—in order to make this source of help and inspiration available to readers of all ages and especially to the young people who must bear the burden of the coming century. To begin, perhaps we might get to know each other better by sharing information about our childhoods.

Pauling: I was born in Portland, Oregon, on February 28, 1901. For the next few years, I lived with my parents in Salem, Portland, and Oswego—all in Oregon. My memories of those places are scant. My main boyhood recollections begin when I was about four years old. At the time, we were living in Condon, Oregon, where we remained a few years. I had long, golden curls, which my father decided to have cut off. No doubt regretting the loss of a baby who was already growing into a boy, when she first saw me after the haircut, my mother burst into tears.

Ikeda: Most mothers share a sentimental regret at seeing their infants begin to show even the first signs of growing up. No doubt, your mother was warmly devoted to her children.

I was born on January 2, 1928, at a place called Iriarai, in Ota

1

Ward, Tokyo. Our neighborhood was in the city. But with its blue skies, sparkling nearby sea, and adjacent fields of seasonally blooming wild flowers it seemed more like a fishing village. Was yours a large family?

Pauling: My father, Herman Henry William Pauling, was a druggist. My mother, Lucy Isabelle Darling Pauling, was the daughter of Linus Wilson Darling, who had a varied career. At different phases in his life he was a school teacher, a rancher, a store keeper, a sheriff, a surveyor, and later a lawyer. My sister Pauline was born in 1902; and my other sister Frances Lucille, in 1904.

Ikeda: My father's name was Nenokichi, and my mother's Ichi. My father was the second son in a family of three sons and five daughters. He and his older brother operated an edible-seaweed company. Your father's profession as druggist probably exerted an influence on your early interest in chemistry.

Pauling: Although he died when I was only nine years old, I remember my father with great affection. His demise left mother in serious financial troubles. She did her best to care for me and my sisters by taking in paying roomers.

Ikeda: Life must have been difficult for a wife and small children deprived of their mainstay at so early a stage in life. My own father lived until I was thirty. His business never really prospered. During World War II our house was burned. But I remember my father as a strong person who, in spite of all tribulations, resolutely persevered in what he thought was right. Furthermore, he was always eager to be of help to others. Reflecting on the situation now, I realize how fine a man he must have been to want to be of assistance when he had financial worries of his own to cope with.

My mother, who lived to be eighty, raised her own eight children plus two that she took in from outside the family. In most respects, she was an ordinary mother, but her life was triumphant in its way.

The faculty of memory seems to vary remarkably among individuals. Some people can recall things that happened at very early ages. The great English historian Arnold J. Toynbee (1889–1975) once told me he could remember events that occurred when he had been only two. In general, Mr. Toynbee stressed early learning and went so far as to say that what a child masters before the age of seven is more important than anything he learns for decades thereafter.

Pauling: I have already mentioned remembering having my long, curly hair cut off when I was four. Some others of my earliest memories include a new pair of boots for tramping through mud puddles in Condon, Oregon. And I recall talking with cowboy loungers in front of the general store my uncle ran.

Ikeda: Were your parents strict?

Pauling: I do not think I received much home discipline. My father and mother taught my sisters and me to behave properly, but I had little tendency to get into trouble. Our home discipline may be described as lenient.

Ikeda: It appears that American parents tend to be lenient. They seem to teach the basics of social living and to respect their children's individual personalities and freedoms. They trust their children, as your parents no doubt did you and your sisters. The traditional Japanese system is far less open and trustful.

Were you robust as a child? I was so frail that doctors sometimes debated the likelihood of my survival. And I too not infrequently shared their mistrust.

Pauling: I was and have generally remained in good health. My sisters recall my having had occasional colds. And, on the basis of a decision taken by my mother and an aunt who was a nurse, I had my tonsils removed when I was twelve. (Tonsillectomies were popular eighty years ago.)

But I was strong and a fast runner. In my first year in college I wanted to be a high-hurdler but was not quite good enough to make the team. A necessary job I had at the time kept me from practicing.

Unforgettable and Irreplaceable

Ikeda: You were fortunate to have been strong and hearty enough to have been good at sports as well as at study. Because of poor health, in my youth, I had to rely largely on support and assistance from others. Now that I am past sixty, I realize all the more vividly the truth of the Buddhist teaching to the effect that we depend on all beings for benevolence. No doubt you too have friends and associates whose support and understanding make them unforgettable and irreplaceable.

Pauling: When I was a boy, William Ziegler, a druggist who had been a friend of my father, helped me in various ways. For example, he gave me chemicals and apparatus for use in study. A neighbor named Mr. Yokum, who had once been a guide on Mount Hood—an extinct volcano in northern Oregon and a popular skiing area—and was then a curator at the North Pacific Dental College, gave me chemical apparatus and an old bicycle and encouraged me to study Greek from books he lent me. (I studied Latin between the ages of twelve and fifteen at Washington High School in Portland.)

Lloyd Alexander Jeffress was my best friend as a boy and throughout his whole life. He became a professor of psychology at the University of Texas in Austin. When I was sixteen, he and his uncle and aunt strongly encouraged me to go on to Oregon Agricultural College to study chemical engineering, although my mother would have preferred me to continue working in a machine shop where I had a job.

Ikeda: And what about teachers who stimulated you or guided you into paths of study that later proved fruitful?

Pauling: During my primary- and secondary-school days, many teachers made significant impressions on me. In the main, they were teachers of mathematics, physics, and chemistry. I remember especially vividly Mr. William Greene, a chemistry teacher at Washington High School. Frequently, toward the end of the school day, he would ask me to remain an extra hour to help him in determining the calorific values of the coal and oil the municipal school board purchased. The year after I had taken his course in chemistry, he allowed me to work in the chemical laboratory by myself and, to my surprise, gave me credit for an extra year of high school chemistry. When I asked him who was the greatest chemist in the world at the time, he said Wilhelm Ostwald, the recognized founder of physical chemistry. Although I believe Ostwald was still living when my wife and I visited Germany in 1926, it never occurred to me to visit him.

Ikeda: I remember with special clarity a certain Mr. Hiyama, who was supervisory teacher when I was in the fifth and sixth years of primary school. He was celebrated for his lectures, but I consider his ability to understand and cultivate the characteristics of individual students far more important. He demonstrated an impressive respect for lively, inquiring, young minds and convinced his students of the need to adhere to high principles. Possibly it was owing to his influence that, after World War II, I became editor of two young-people's magazines published by my mentor Josei Toda, who was the second president of Soka Gakkai and a person of the most decisive importance to me.

Lamentably, education today often seems to lack the kind of personal warmth you experienced from Mr. Greene and I enjoyed from Mr. Hiyama. This is all the more regrettable since teachers can determine the courses students' whole lives will follow.

Upon completing high-school work, you went on to study at Oregon Agricultural College, in Corvallis. Does this mean that your pecuniary problems had been resolved?

Pauling: No. The family financial situation was still difficult. Even while still well, my mother clearly was unable to finance college for me. Still I wanted to go on with my studies. And, because I had done well in school, my friends urged me to continue.

Doing odd jobs of one sort or another, I was able to make my way and even send some money to mother. Between my second and third years, however, her needs became so pressing that I took a year off from study to work full time, first as a paving engineer on a highway and then as an instructor at Oregon Agricultural College. This enabled me to send money home.

Ikeda: Although your circumstances were hard, your successes substantiate my belief in the need for young people to know what hard work means. When times were trying for our family, I too worked—for instance, as a newspaper boy for three years beginning in the sixth year of primary school. When my own sons entered college, I told them to find part-time jobs and not to rely entirely on their parents. Still, as long as conditions permit, promising young people ought to have opportunities to prepare themselves to lead active, productive adult lives, as you did—in spite of hardships—at college. Your university years must have been of the greatest importance to you.

Pauling: It is difficult to evaluate my college experience. Routine outside work took time away from my studies. And this may have been detrimental. Until I was given a part-time job at the university, I spent a hundred hours a month working elsewhere. This meant three hours a day chopping wood or performing some other kind of labor. Still, because it accustomed me to long hours of hard work, this experience may actually have been profitable.

Ikeda: Knowledge of the meaning of work stands us all in good stead, as it most assuredly did you. I often advise young people to seek out work deliberately for the sake of self-development. Even work that seems grueling at the time usually comes to be recognized later as having had some value—physical or psychological.

Pauling: The nature of the school I attended may have had something to do with later developments. In 1940, my friend the American physicist Harold Uray (1893–1981), who won a Nobel Prize for chemistry in 1934, said that he and I may have been fortunate in going to colleges with no very high level of academic achievement. In such environments, we stood out among our classmates—he was the best student, and I was among the best. Being outstanding in this way gave us confidence of success.

Ikeda: Do you mean, like being a big frog in a little pond? An oriental proverb says it is better to be the head of a chicken than the rump of a cow (that is, to be the leader of a small group than to be a follower in a large one). I am certain that such self-evaluation from a man with your record of brilliant achievements would surprise many people. How else did the nature of your college influence you?

Pauling: Our university environment did have one other important effect on me. When I was there, Oregon Agricultural College
offered only elementary mathematics courses and calculus. After I got
to the California Institute of Technology (in 1922), I was eager to fill
the gap in my mathematical education. This is why my doctor's degree
was not in chemistry alone. I did so much study in mathematics and
physics that the faculty awarded me a doctorate—*summa cum laude*
too—in mathematical physics.

Ikeda: During your long association with the California Institute
of Technology and in your extensive scholarly and later pacifist spheres
of acquaintance, you must have met many people who impressed and
influenced you.

Pauling: Several great teachers exerted a decisive influence on
my scientific life. Among them were Roscoe Gilkey Dickinson and
Richard Chace Tolman, of the California Institute of Technology.

Dickinson, who was only ten years my senior, was the first person
to be awarded a Ph.D. from the California Institute of Technology. He
was doing research on X-ray diffraction by crystals and determining
crystal structures. I began working with him immediately after arriving
at the institute in September, 1922.

A very thoughtful, careful person, he taught me how to think about
experiments and their results and how to analyze them to determine
whether advance assumptions had been made and how to evaluate the
reliability of conclusions. Of course, he taught me experimental methods as well.

Richard Chace Tolman, a remarkable man with a good knowledge
of physics and mathematics as well as of chemistry, taught me a great
deal about scientific discovery, research, and the nature of science
itself.

In later years, I came to work with the distinguished German
scholar Professor Arnold Sommerfeld at the University of Munich—
first for the year of 1926–27 and then again for three or four months
in 1930. His thorough teaching method and the excellence of his lectures were very impressive. I learned a great deal from him.

In a somewhat different connection, I might mention Albert
Schweitzer. My wife and I were invited (in 1959) to visit his medical
mission in Lambarené, Gabon, where we spent about two weeks. After

the first two or three days, Dr. Schweitzer began asking me to join him in the evening after dinner for about an hour's conversation. He spoke with my wife too, but only at the dinner table. In this respect, he was more old-fashioned than Albert Einstein, who always asked my wife to take part in our discussions. Dr. Schweitzer and I talked mostly about world affairs and the radiation caused by nuclear testing. He impressed me very greatly; and, as I recall, we concurred on everything.

As you know, on April 24, 1957, Albert Schweitzer made a radio broadcast entitled "Declaration of Conscience" from Oslo, Norway. In it, he spoke frankly of the danger of radiation from nuclear weapons tests not only to the environment and the health of living people, but also to the health of coming generations resulting from damage done to reproductive cells. He called for an expression of informed public opinion in all nations that would compel statesmen to agree to stop bomb tests and, after urging humanity to find the courage to "leave folly and face reality," concluded by saying, "The end of further experiments with atom bombs would be like the early sun rays of hope which suffering humanity is longing for."

In the spirit that inspired his radio broadcast, Dr. Schweitzer signed the "Petition to the United Nations Urging That an International Agreement to Stop the Testing of Nuclear Bombs Be Made Now." Indeed, I believe he signed it three times: each time he came upon a copy, he would sign it and mail it to me. My wife and I presented this petition, signed by 9,235 scientists, including numerous Nobel Prize laureates, to Mr. Dag Hammarskjold, then secretary general of the United Nations, on Monday, January 15, 1958.

Ikeda: Of course, work for peace was only one of the many tasks in which Albert Schweitzer concerned himself. The late Norman Cousins, of the University of California in Los Angeles, once told me that Dr. Schweitzer insisted that the best cure for any illness is a combination of knowledge of the task in hand and a sense of humor. Professor Cousins also told me that Schweitzer often remarked to his close working associates, "I'm not going to die as long as I have work to do. If there's work, there's no need to die. That's why I'm going to live a long time." And, of course, he did live to be ninety.

Although various evaluations have been made of his legacy, I am deeply impressed by Dr. Schweitzer's determination always to make the best of his own potentialities. Do you have other recollections of him?

Pauling: Once, for a day or two, he lent me the scrapbooks in which he pasted newspaper clippings on world affairs together with his own annotations. Personal contact substantiated and verified the high opinion I and most other people had of Dr. Schweitzer. He was devoted to improving the physical conditions in which black people lived, though he clearly did not consider them his equals and made little effort to improve their education or alter their life styles.

Ikeda: Who else has made an especially strong impression on you?

Pauling: Of course, I had great respect for Bertrand Russell. Since his interests were mathematics and philosophy and mine were physics and chemistry, we did not discuss science much. Nonetheless I admire the stands he took.

The many impressive people with whom I have become acquainted in the Soviet Union, Germany, France, and other countries are too numerous to list. But the person who was my greatest teacher in the broad aspects of life was my wife.

Ava Helen Pauling

Ikeda: Your wife, Ava Helen Pauling, worked together with you in the cause of peace for many years. Your reference to her as one of your most important teachers indicates the profound relation you two shared.

Josei Toda, whom I have already mentioned, exerted the strongest influence on my decision to devote myself to the cause of peace. In addition to being a genius at mathematics, he was widely learned in many other fields, including, of course, Buddhism. His erudition extended to social sciences, natural sciences, and analysis of world conditions. He instructed me in all these things and in organizational management and even in questions related to managing my personal life. Instead of merely imparting knowledge, he imbued in me philosophical attitudes and down-to-earth wisdom that remain with me to the present. I have heard it said that education is what is left when one has forgotten everything learned in schools. What I gained from Mr. Toda was education of this kind.

In many instances home life plays a tremendously important role in educating young people in the attitudes and skills of social and family life. I am certain that your wife's contribution to the education of your children—all of whom are now outstanding members of American society—was especially great.

Pauling: I suspect that I made no special effort to spend the maximum amount of time with our four children. I left the major part of child upbringing to my wife. Once in a while, I played baseball with them; but, in this respect, I was not an especially good father.

At one time, I thought I would try to help my eldest son advance more rapidly in school by instructing him in elementary algebra. But this attempt turned out unsuccessfully. He was interested in learning only what his teachers taught him. And I immediately abandoned the idea of giving my children academic instruction. Of course, both my wife and I always discussed world affairs and good behavior with the children, who were probably brought up to have good moral principles.

Ikeda: Children pattern themselves on their parents. An industrious and vigorous approach to life impresses them much more deeply than any amount of preaching. Realizing the effect adult conversation and behavior have, I advocate respecting the individualities of young people by acting and speaking on their levels. Your example and that of your wife no doubt provided great inspiration for your children.

In addition to child-rearing and domestic management, your wife was of significant assistance to you in your public life.

Pauling: I have so many memories of my wife that it is hard to know where to begin talking about the ways she helped me. I distinctly remember the first time I ever saw her. I had been asked to instruct a class of twenty-five girls in first-year college chemistry. After introducing myself as the instructor, I selected a name at random from my class roster and asked the girl questions. The girl was Ava Helen Miller, who later became my wife.

At the time, I was impressed by her wide knowledge and interest in many subjects, including world affairs. She was majoring in home economics and, I am sure, had already set as her goal the development of a successful family. For many years, she devoted herself to taking care of me and our children.

Ikeda: In the life of any man who wants to do his own work well, a wife plays a vital role. Because I am extremely busy, my wife conducts all domestic affairs almost as if I were absent from the scene.

As Buddhism teaches, suffering is inherent in human life. Inevitably we must all lose people who are close to us. When your mother died, you were already married and well advanced on the road to your future successes.

Pauling: Yes, I was married. In 1926, my wife and I were traveling and were in Munich when a letter arrived from my sister saying mother had died. There were guests in the room at the time, but after opening and reading the letter, I burst into tears.

My father's death had occurred when I was too young to understand. But I grasped the significance of mother's dying and was especially sorrowful because I knew she had been disappointed in me for remaining in school on scholarships instead of earning a good living. I had hoped that one day she would come to understand and appreciate what I was trying to do. Her death dashed that hope. Five years later, when I received the Langmuir Prize as the most promising young chemist in the United States, I wished mother had still been alive.

Ikeda: Understandably, you wanted your mother to see your dreams come true. It is tragic that she never witnessed your triumphs. Still your great achievements are the finest tribute you could pay to her memory.

You and your wife were young when you were married. So were my wife and I. We were young but not irresponsible. The French writer André Maurois once said that marriages are happy if, at proposal time, both parties sincerely intend to make their union last. My wife and I sincerely intended our marriage to last, and it has. Of course, we realized that hardships are part of life, but we vowed to help each other as much as possible.

Pauling: Young men and women must strive to find and marry the right person early. My wife was nineteen and I was twenty-two when we married. We had wanted to marry the year before, but practical considerations prevented us. I was fortunate in having been selected by the right young woman.

My wife was happy making a home for me and the children. Later she found considerable happiness in being a public figure active in such causes as human rights and world peace.

Ikeda: In this connection her work partly corresponded with your own. In all of your varied interests have you been guided by any single principle that might be summarized in something like a motto? When I asked him a similar question, Arnold J. Toynbee characteristically replied that his personal motto was the single Latin word *Laboramus*, or "let us work," which was the word-for-the-day given just prior to his death by the Roman emperor Septimus Severus.

Curiosity About the Universe

Pauling: Perhaps I have no motto as such. But since my youth, I have wanted to learn as much as possible about the world. As a child, I enjoyed reading and going to school. My early interest in learning developed into an extreme curiosity about the nature of the universe. That curiosity remains my main driving force.

Ikeda: Your curiosity is, of course, the scientist's characteristic inquiring spirit. If, as Plato contended, amazement is the driving force of philosophy, insatiable curiosity is the origin of all learning.

Active from your youth, you were entrusted with positions of responsibility at a very young age. Were they ever difficult to cope with?

Pauling: I recognized rather early that I was doing good work in chemistry. At the age of thirty-six, I was appointed chairman of the Division of Chemistry and Chemical Engineering and director of the Gates and Crellin Laboratories of Chemistry. I considered this appointment proper because, as was clear both to me and to others, I had been making important contributions to chemistry. But I always wanted to continue working with my students and associates in ways that would most effectively promote learning more about the nature of the universe.

Once in charge of the Division of Chemistry and Chemical Engineering, I decided not to make all decisions myself but to encourage the active participation of my fellow professors. My policy of delegating authority and of not interfering in the ways they exercised it left me free to devote most of my time and energy to solving scientific problems.

Ikeda: Your attitude demonstrates concern for harmonious human relations and magnanimous generosity and sets a fine example for young people today.

You have consistently displayed astonishing energy, even at a time in life when other less vigorous people might be thinking of retiring from active work. For instance, you were over sixty years old when you began research on vitamin C. To what do you attribute this vitality?

Pauling: Changes in interest have stimulated me greatly. Approximately every ten years, a significant change has occurred in the direction of my scientific work. In about 1930, I switched from the study of minerals and other inorganic compounds to research in organic molecules. In about 1935, I developed an interest in the structure of proteins and other macromolecules present in the human body. In 1936, I began working on the problem of the nature of antibodies and of serological reactions. Then, in 1945, I developed the idea that such a thing as molecular disease might exist and formulated a theory about sickle-cell anemia as such a disease. In 1965, after having studied the problem of their nature for some decades, I developed a new theory about atomic nuclei. In about 1965, I grew curious about vitamins and, in 1968, formulated the basic principles of what is now called ortho-molecular medicine, according to which diseases may be cured by restoring certain substances already present in the body, to optimal levels.

Over the decades, I have built up a tremendous body of knowledge about the nature of the universe—or at least of what may be called the physical universe—in all its aspects. In the many books and journals I read, whenever I come across a statement that surprises me or attracts my interest, I ask whether it fits into the picture of the universe I have formulated. If it fits, I am satisfied. If not, I ask, first, whether the statement might be wrong or, second, if it is right, whether it might provide a basis for obtaining additional information about the structure of the universe. As a consequence of thinking along these lines, I have been able to formulate a number of new ideas and to add gradually to my understanding.

Ikeda: Curiosity is mental youth. Newton's famous words suggest an image of the scientist as a child constantly pursuing the novel:

> I do not know what I may appear to the world, but to myself I seem to have been only a boy playing on the seashore, and diverting myself in now and then finding a smoother pebble or a prettier shell than the ordinary, whilst the great ocean of truth lay all undiscovered before me.

This kind of mental youthfulness is discernible, not only in scientists, but also in all people who do outstanding work and, even when physically old, remain profoundly curious and sensitive.

Henry Kissinger once told me that scientists become increasingly humble with each new discovery that brings them closer to the truth about the universe. All of us would do well to adopt a similar attitude of humble reverence in the face of the universe. No matter how great it might seem, the knowledge of the moment is never more than a small part of the mysterious totality of the knowable.

Your own search for the truth of the universe has been rewarded with two Nobel prizes, the chemistry award in 1954 and the peace award in 1962. How did you react to these honors?

Two Nobel Prizes

Pauling: When I received notice that I had been awarded the Nobel Prize for Chemistry for 1954, I was pleased but not really surprised because rumor of its coming to me had been abroad for some time. I knew that my many investigations into the chemical bond and the structures of complex substances were important and had changed the nature of chemistry during the preceding twenty-five years. The Nobel Prize was given to me for doing work I enjoyed: satisfying my curiosity about the natures of crystals, gas molecules, and other substances.

I place much higher value on the Nobel Prize for Peace, for 1962, which was awarded to me on October 10, 1963. It was a great surprise. At the time, I said my having received it made working for peace respectable. Of course, my wife, my children, and I had all suffered considerably during the years of our pacifist work.

Ikeda: In your 1963 Nobel Lecture, you said,

"I believe that there will never again be a great world war—a war in which the terrible weapons involving nuclear fission and nuclear fusion would be used. And I believe that it is the discoveries of scientists upon which the development of these terrible weapons was based that are now forcing us to move into a new period in the history of the world, a period of peace and reason, when world problems are solved in accordance with world law, in a way that does justice to all nations and benefits all people."

By consistently demanding the abolition of war, you have greatly encouraged pacifists everywhere. In your peace-related work, you have traveled all over the world, visiting forty-two countries, including Japan. I understand that you are no longer interested in traveling and prefer to spend your time working in peace at your home in Big Sur, California. How do you arrange your days there?

Pauling: My wife and I acquired 100 hectares of land in Big Sur in 1955. The small cabin that was on it then is gone now. We built a house on the land twenty-three years ago as a place for our retirement. Of course, I still have not retired; but I spend more time in that house than anywhere else. It is where I do my scientific work. I am alone there half the time. At the Linus Pauling Institute of Science and Medicine, in Palo Alto, I discuss various activities, answer letters, and do a little administrative work. Although I am involved in some experimental projects there, I only supervise.

At Big Sur, where there are no nearby friends or theaters, I have little to do in the evening and customarily go to bed at about eight o'clock. I wake at about four—sometimes even three—in the morning, have breakfast, and start work.

To an extent, the climate accounts for my early schedule. In our part of California, it is apt to be cold at night and warm in the daytime. On clear days, the sun shines into the house and keeps it comfortable. I build a fire in the morning when I get up, work in front of the fireplace, and then let the fire go out. If I were to work into the evening, I would have to build another fire. I do not want to do that and go to bed early instead.

Ikeda: You have published an immense number of works on chemistry, physics, molecular biology, and medicine in the past and today still publish on theoretical chemistry. How many written works do you have to your credit? Which of them do you consider most important?

Pauling: I have published about six hundred scientific papers and about two hundred papers on world affairs. Not counting translations, I have published perhaps twenty books. About five of them are on orthomolecular medicine, and two, *No More War* and *Science and Peace*, are about the pacifist movement.

In a sense, I am proudest of my work for world peace, because it has made a significant contribution to all humanity by helping reduce damage done by nuclear tests and stimulating action in the direction of eliminating war.

Some people claim that I shall probably be remembered as the vitamin C man. I am rather glad to have been effective in stimulating people to take large doses of that vitamin. I regret doctors' reluctance to accept this as a way of helping control cancer and hope they will someday incorporate it in their therapy.

If I were to choose for myself, I should like to be remembered as the person who discovered hybridization of orbitals (the subject of a paper I wrote in 1931). I believe my work on developing the modern theory of the chemical bond has been my greatest contribution to science.

Ikeda: Inspiration is often said to be essential to the kind of brilliant scientific research you were already conducting in your twenties and thirties. Have you found instinct and inspiration important in your work?

Pauling: It depends on what the word *inspiration* is taken to mean. I once knew a physical chemist who was interested in what he called hunches. A hunch is a kind of inspiration: a new idea that suddenly occurs to the mind. In a paper he presented to the National Academy of Sciences of the United States, this scientist reported on having asked one hundred chemists about their hunches. Four or five people failed to understand his meaning, but many of the chemists interviewed agreed that they sometimes acted on hunches.

I have written a paper and delivered an address on the genesis of ideas and have said that hunches, or inspirations, come to me often when I have thought about a problem for years and then have suddenly found the answer. This is because I train my subconscious mind to retain and ponder problems. Whenever a new idea enters my head, my subconscious mind asks whether it is related to any of the long-standing problems stored there. If there is a connection, the new material is brought to the attention of my conscious mind. This way of thinking is not unique with me.

Ikeda: Thomas Edison said genius is ninety-nine percent perspiration and one percent inspiration. Anyone could have seen an apple fall from a tree, but only Newton had the accumulated knowledge and reflective abilities to deduce the universal law of gravitation from this simple phenomenon. The falling apple brought to full fruition things that had long been active in Newton's subconscious mind.

Pauling: Investigators in the field of inspirations, or hunches, have suggested that a person who commands several branches of knowledge transfers something that is well-known in one area into other areas. The act of transferral constitutes an inspiration. I think this is true.

Not all the many ideas I have had about science have proved correct; nonetheless, I have discovered many things and have published my discoveries. This is probably because I think more about scientific problems than most other scientists. Another reason is my broad background of knowledge. This scope enables me to transfer facts from the field of physics to chemical problems to which they have never been applied before. This process can be rather straightforward, but some of my ideas have been somewhat more inspirational (I do not mean in the sense that the spirit breathed them into me). My inspirational ideas have come from my great body of knowledge.

Ikeda: Your example of new ideas rising from a large body of learning calls to mind a serious problem confronting modern civilization; that is, how to harmonize individual items of knowledge with total wisdom. Rapid expansion of the information-oriented society has vastly increased the amount of informational data available to everyone. Most of this information, however, consists of isolated items. As acquisition of information becomes an end in itself, goals for the convergence of all information fade from view. When this happens, items of knowledge remain isolated from each other like the pieces of a scattered jigsaw puzzle.

Instead of being conducive to human well-being, floods of such data can actually be harmful. This is why we rely on people like you, with broad stores of knowledge and great intellectual powers, to co-ordinate information within a larger pattern of wisdom.

As I have said, when I was young, conditions in Japan made serious study difficult. But my mentor Josei Toda insisted that I—and all other young people too—must set aside time for reading and serious speculation. As I followed his advice, books became my friends and my spiritual sustenance. I took notes on everything I read.

Pauling: I too read a great many books when I was a boy. When I had just turned nine, my father wrote a letter to a morning newspaper—the *Oregonian* in Portland—stating that I had already read the Bible and Darwin's *Origin of Species*. When I was about twelve, I occasionally went to visit my uncle Judge James Ulysses Campbell and his wife and daughter. While with them, I spent all my time reading the eleventh edition of the *Encyclopedia Britannica*. I remember reading books on ancient history and *Alice in Wonderland* and *Through the Looking Glass*. Examining a Doré illustrated edition of Dante's *Inferno* when I was about ten made me skeptical about revealed religion.

Ikeda: Early impressions like the one of the Doré illustrations to Dante's great poem often persist for a lifetime. That is why influences made on young minds are of the greatest importance. Though they should be responsible for a large part of cultivating children, contemporary education systems are often criticized for the poor job they do. Public education faces many problems in the United States. And, in Japan, excessive emphasis on the mere imparting of information and on test scores means that cultivation of the all-round human being is often neglected. Reflecting on your own background, how would you evaluate the system under which you were educated? What aspects of the modern educational system require revision?

Pauling: The education I received seventy-five years ago in the elementary schools of Oregon, a state with a small population, was really excellent. Although I am no longer in close touch with teaching in the United States, elementary school education today may not be as good as it should be.

Everyone who wants to further his education should have the opportunity to do so at any time in life. Soon technological advances and automation will free us of the necessity of devoting fifty or sixty years to jobs providing no satisfaction. With the consequent increases in leisure time they will enjoy, people should be afforded ample opportunity to improve themselves through study.

At the present time, however, opportunities to do so are restricted. In Japan, the number of universities is insufficient to accommodate all the young people who want to learn. In the United States, university education is often prohibitively expensive—even to people who would greatly benefit by it. The pressing need is to understand that we must provide opportunities for a higher education to all who want one.

Ikeda: I agree entirely. Your advocacy of education for all who need it reflects the same humanism that is evident in your work for the global-peace movement and your concern to protect human health. Your attitude relates closely to the Buddhist practice of regarding the suffering of others as one's own suffering and desiring to eliminate it. As a Buddhist, I have been greatly impressed by your humanistic activities.

Being a Humanist

Pauling: Being a humanist means working for the benefit of human beings and, perhaps, for the prevention of suffering in animals as well. *The American Humanist* once selected me as Humanist of the Year, and I submitted a paper to them. In it I spoke of a basic ethical principle that can be derived by means of scientific argument. That principle is minimizing human suffering. Living in accordance with this principle means behaving towards others as we would like them to behave towards us. This, of course, is a basic ethical tenet of most great religions.

Ikeda: Your concise statement of the principle recalls Kant's famous philosophy of the individual. He prized above everything the self-controlling operations of the free character. In his *Grundlegung zur Metaphysik der Sitten* "Foundation of the metaphysics of morals", Kant said that the same human nature is present in all individual characters and that we must always act in such a way that our human nature is an end and never a mere means. A retrospective view of the gory exploitations and degradations of human dignity that constitute the history of our race ought to send us hurrying back to reread Kant's thoughts on this topic.

Interestingly, the oriental version of the humanistic principle of doing unto others as we should have them do unto us is expressed inversely by Confucius:

What you do not want done to yourself, do not do to others.

—*The Analects of Confucius*

Pauling: In my paper in *The American Humanist*, after stating my belief in the ethical principle derived according to scientific methods, I expressed my rejection of bias and dogma. I have, in fact, rejected both since childhood.

I must have become an atheist at a fairly young age. I do not believe in the existence of God. The problems associated with the nature of God and the reasons why he is able to behave as he does make me see no advantage in such belief. I am not, however, militant in my atheism.

The great English theoretical physicist Paul Dirac is a militant atheist. I suppose he is interested in arguing about the existence of God. I am not. It was once quipped that there is no God and Dirac is his prophet.

I am a humanist. In addition, I am a member of the Unitarian Church of Los Angeles. In 1961, the Unitarians and the Universalists joined to form the Unitarian Universalist Association, which accepts people of all faiths and is by no means a Christian organization. The Unitarians were once considered Christian and published a journal called *The Christian Monthly;* but the name has been changed to *The Unitarian Universalist Monthly*. My wife and I joined the Los Angeles Unitarian Church some years ago because it accepts as members people who believe in trying to make the world a better place.

Ikeda: I find your rejection of bias and dogma very interesting. The problem of these two is at least as old as Greek philosophy and its distinction between *episteme* "knowledge" and *doxa* "opinion." Religions must make every effort to avoid both bias and dogma. If they fail in this, they lose the ability to establish a sound humanism and can even distort human nature. The twenty-first century has no need of religions of this kind.

The West has frequently witnessed keen opposition between the advocates of faith and those of reason. The early Christian writer Tertullian (c. 160–230) put the situation concisely when he said that we have faith in some things precisely because they are irrational.

The dichotomy between faith and reason seems to be limited generally to the sphere of Christian influence. And, even there, a catholic balance has often existed between them, though a religio-scientific conflict has raged, on and off, for centuries.

In other cultural spheres—Islamic, Indian, Chinese, and so on—conciliation and mutual assistance have tended to characterize relations between faith and reason, religion and science. This is as it should be since broadly philosophical religion and science are both essential elements in human life.

In Buddhist thought there is no conflict between reason and faith. In the world as postulated by Buddhist philosophy, the operations of unaided knowledge have been exhausted and knowledge realizes its own limitations. Explained in other words, this realm is one in which the intellect is capable of criticizing itself. Only a faith in which intellect and reason unite to reinforce each other can serve as the core of true humanism. Such a religion has much in common with what Einstein may have meant when he said,

> I maintain that cosmic religious feeling is the strongest and noblest incitement to scientific research.
>
> —Albert Einstein, *The World as I See It*

Leaving the broad, cosmic scale for a while, I should like to deal briefly with the question of individual happiness. Generally people interpret happiness in terms of health, economic security, social position, and so on. At the present time, however, we seem to be witnessing a shift in emphasis from the material to the spiritual. People are tending more and more to interpret satisfaction of the mind and the knowledge that one's life is meaningful to others as the best criteria of happiness.

Happiness

Pauling: Different people have different views of happiness. I consider true happiness to be a sense of satisfaction in living. I should like for everyone to be able to enjoy the wonders of the world and to have leisure and money to travel and find enjoyment in many ways. Everyone should have adequate food, housing, and clothing; the degree of education his needs require; and—most important—the kind of job that brings him satisfaction.

As far as women are concerned, I am old-fashioned enough to like the idea of a woman's managing the household. This is an important activity. A woman does not have to be a bank vice-president to find happiness. I should think routine work like sitting at a desk writing letters, making reports, or punching data into computers would be much less interesting and satisfying than running a home.

Ikeda: The Lotus Sutra teaches that the present world is one in which sentient beings should amuse and enjoy themselves. In this context, *amuse* means, not superficial pleasure, but the sense of satisfaction that you say is essential to happiness. With all due respect to the noble aims of the movement, in concerning themselves too much with equality, some advocates of woman's liberation either have lost sight of or have underestimated the happiness a woman can find in caring for husband, children, and home.

A certain Japanese philosopher was once distressed to observe that a noted book on ethics completely ignored the matter of happiness. Perhaps the lives of many people today are equally indifferent to this important topic. The frequency of marital failures indicated by rising divorce rates suggest that, at least, happiness often proves elusive.

The Japanese people are frequently accused of being workaholics. This does not necessarily mean that they find great mental or spiritual satisfaction in their tasks, many of which are drudgery or mere business. It seems likely that Japanese fathers and husbands sometimes sacrifice potentially enriching family and home life to jobs that bring no true gratification at all. If this is the case, such men illustrate the meaning of an old proverb about the folly of straightening a cow's horns and killing the animal in the process. In other words, they are destroying something of value for the sake of tasks scarcely worth the performing.

2

Science and Humanity

Is the Possibility of Learning Limited?

Ikeda: What motivated you to choose science as your field of endeavor?

Pauling: When I was eleven years old, from reading, I became interested in entomology. For a year, I made a small collection of insects. Then, when I was twelve, my interest turned to mineralogy. I had little opportunity to collect minerals, except agates, which were plentiful in the Willamette Valley; but I read books and copied tables of mineral properties. When I was thirteen, I turned my attention to chemistry and have remained interested in it all my life.

Ikeda: By introducing quantum mechanics, your theory of the chemical bond virtually reformed traditional chemistry. What are your opinions of the fundamental nature of chemistry and the contributions it can make to humanity?

Pauling: The knowledge of electrons, nuclei, atoms, and molecules developed during the last one hundred years has brought chemistry and physics so close together that it is now difficult to distinguish between them. The goal of both is to understand the world as thoroughly as possible. I have been especially interested in relations between the compositions and structures of substances and their properties. About ten million different substances have been discovered or created by chemists and other scientists, and many of their properties have been described. Their structures are now so well understood that chemists and physicists can sometimes predict the kinds of substances that must be produced in order to achieve certain desirable properties. The modern world has been shaped by discoveries made by physicists and chemists during the last century or two. As long as politicians and other people in power refrain from hindering them, these scientists can continue contributing to the well-being of all peoples.

Ikeda: The quantum theory states that systems can gain or lose energy only in discrete amounts called quanta. Quantum mechanics, a formulation of early thoughts developed from this theory, has been used to explain atomic and nuclear phenomena. It is sometimes referred to as the science closest to philosophy. What future developments do you foresee for quantum mechanics?

Pauling: In my opinion, quantum mechanics is essentially a practical subject. Just as Newton's laws of motion have permitted calculation of the paths followed not only by the heavenly bodies, but also by space ships, so quantum mechanics permits reliable calculations about electrons and atoms. Although it has not yet been incorporated finally into the theory of relativity and other physical theories, in the course of time, such integration will be achieved.

Ikeda: I posed the preceding question because of the vivid impression made on me by the book *Physics and Beyond* by the German leading light in the field of quantum mechanics, Werner Karl Heisenberg (1901–1976), whose work overturned conventional physics. As is pointed out by the Japanese nuclear physicist and Nobel Prize laureate Hideki Yukawa (1907–1981), the contents of Heisenberg's books are highly philosophical. For example, its chapters bear such titles as "Quantum Mechanics and the Philosophy of Kant" and "Particles and Platonic Philosophy." About the relation of part and whole, Heisenberg says,

> We can objectify no more than a small part of our world. But even when we try to probe into the subjective realm, we cannot ignore

the central order or look upon the forms peopling this realm as mere phantoms or accidents. Admittedly, the subjective realm of an individual, no less than a nation, may sometimes be in a state of confusion. Demons can be let loose and do a great deal of mischief, or, to put it more scientifically, partial orders that have split away from the central order, or do not fit into it, may have taken over. But in the final analysis, the central order, or the "one" as it used to be called and with which we commune in the language of religion, must win out. And when people search for values, they are probably searching for the kind of actions that are in harmony with the central order, and as such are free of the confusions springing from the divided, partial orders.

—Werner Heisenberg, *Physics and Beyond*

This passage describes the harmony created by the unions of the subjective and the objective, of humanity, nature, and the universe. In another passage, Heisenberg adds a comment to the effect that our link with the central order has become much more obvious since we have come to understand the quantum theory. Science has already made immense progress. What is your opinion of its future outlook? Is there to be an end to what research can uncover? Certain elementary particles were once considered the ultimate of matter. But gradually more and more particles have been discovered. Putting them in order resulted in the quark theory. For a while, quarks and leptons were thought to represent the ultimate form of matter, but now we hear discussion of a subquark stage. In the light of these changes, we must ask ourselves whether an ultimate boundary will one day be reached. Or will it become necessary to replace the notion of stages of development with some new concept?

Pauling: It is astonishing how much scientists have learned about the laws governing the physical and even the biological world during the past century or century and a half. Every year something new is discovered about the universe. Nevertheless scientists discuss the possibility of an end to further discovery. If the human race and civilization survive a thousand or ten thousand years, will civilized humanity be able to continue developing science? Will all laws of nature ultimately be discovered? I do not know the answer. Some physicists say there is no limit to the discovery of elementary particles. We progressed from the stage at which we knew of only the electron and the nucleus to the stage where we understood the electron, the proton, and the neutron, and from there to the stages of various mesons. Now we know of several hundred elementary particles. I cannot say whether there will be an end to the search.

Earth and Planets Other Than Earth

Ikeda: A discussion I once had with the world-famous American astronomer and author Carl Sagan touched on the search for intelligent extraterrestrial life. From the viewpoint of astronomy, it seems possible that in our galaxy alone there may be ten million planets on which intelligent life can have attained a level of civilization at least as high as our own. In his best-selling book *Cosmos*, Sagan has used equations to arrive at an astonishing number of possibilities. Only recently, the English astronomer Nalin Chandra Wickramasinghe, who teaches at University College, Cardiff, told me it is entirely conceivable that manlike intelligence exists elsewhere in the vastness of the universe and that such beings may well have emerged at a time when life on Earth was still in a primitive stage. Although cosmic science is not my field, as a Buddhist I am interested in views of the universe and life. Do you believe in the possibility of beings with humanlike intelligence on planets other than Earth?

Pauling: The number of stars in the known universe is so great that many of them are certain to be similar to our sun and to have planets, similar to Earth, revolving around them. It is my opinion that living organisms have developed on many of those planets. It is likely that a large number, perhaps all, of such living organisms are based on the element carbon, as life on Earth is. It is, however, unlikely that they will have developed so much like us that we could call them human beings. The development of intelligent beings on other planets seems conceivable, although the number of planets on which human beings have evolved and continued to exist during a period overlapping with our own is probably small.

Ikeda: I was especially interested to hear Professor Wickrama-singhe say we cannot reject the possibility that, after death, human beings might begin other intelligent lives on some other planet. This idea is similar to the Buddhist teaching of reincarnation. In the years to come, the physical sciences will no doubt elucidate the manner in which life emerged on this planet. What is your opinion on the topic?

Pauling: I believe that life emerged on Earth as a logical result of the ability of some molecules to act as catalysts for self-replicating reactions. The molecular interpretation of Darwin's principles of evolution provides an acceptable theory for the origin of life.

Ikeda: In his book *Chance and Necessity*, the French molecular biologist Jacques Monod, who won a Nobel Prize in 1965, said that the emergence of life on Earth was unique in the universe and governed completely by chance. What do you think of his idea?

Pauling: I have read the book you mention and, although I do not disagree with Monod, I think I would amplify his explanation. Correctly interpreted, chance may or may not have significant consequences in chemical reaction; that is, in one aspect of chemistry. Self-replicating events or autocatalytic processes—processes that select and accelerate themselves—could have caused results to accumulate on Earth to the extent that living organisms evolved. In other words, essentially, I can see Monod's point.

Society Must Decide

Ikeda: Molecular biology has advanced to the stage at which it is possible to alter genetic information contained in deoxyribonucleic acid (DNA). Techniques of genetic alteration and cellular fusion constitute the field known as genetic engineering, which poses many problems demanding solution and entailing potential dangers. What is your opinion of the guidelines research workers in the field are establishing for themselves?

Pauling: About ten years ago, geneticists expended great effort trying to determine the hazards genetic engineering represents for humanity. They came to the conclusion that certain controls would suffice to eliminate danger essentially. As is true with all development, however, society itself must decide how to use scientific discoveries for the benefit and not to the detriment (as in war) of humankind.

Ikeda: I agree entirely. We must exercise the greatest possible caution. Without permitting developments in the name of scientific interest alone to get out of hand, we must be as careful as the man in the Japanese proverb who refuses to cross even a stone bridge without tapping on it to ascertain its soundness.

Standards set for genetic engineering in the United States represent an instance in which scientists themselves guide experimentation. Although, at a later date, their controls may turn out to have been too strict, scientists must always examine their work from the standpoint of the general good of humanity and the ecological system.

The major threat to the environment from genetic engineering is the danger of harmful microorganisms. No serious problem has yet arisen in this connection because the activities of those few scientists whose experiments violate established rules are speedily made known to the public. Abiding by regulations adopted for the general good is a matter of the scientist's conscience.

Another trouble point, which is still hypothetical because nothing in this direction has yet been achieved, is the possible ecological influences of the creation of heretofore unknown life forms.

In addition, ethical issues are certain to emerge when biological genetic technology is applied in medical science. Safety must come first. Beyond safety, however, we must question the extent to which manipulating human genetics is justifiable.

Scientists themselves have posed these problems and must bear them constantly in mind in the future. Not everything related to the application of science for the benefit of humanity ought to be left entirely in the hands of scientists. Society at large must play its part. When genetic engineering is put to use on human beings, in addition to scientific opinion, the ideas of representatives of the general public and of the fields of philosophy, anthropology, ethics, and religion must be taken into consideration in all decision-making.

Some scientists in the past have been strongly critical of their own work. The well-known Russell-Einstein Declaration of 1955 embodied the wishes of its originators that scientists—the original creators of nuclear weapons—take the lead in the drive for peace and the abolition of nuclear arms. In 1957, the first of the Pugwash Conferences (named for Pugwash, Nova Scotia, where the meeting was held) was convened to give scientists from all over the world the opportunity of working for peace. You were an influential participant in those conferences. What is your attitude now toward the scientist's responsibility to society?

Pauling: Almost all great world problems have significant scientific content. For half a century, I have contended that scientists have the special duty of helping their fellow citizens make the right decisions by assisting in educating them about the scientific aspects of problems and by expressing their own opinions.

Reasonableness and a Great Sense of Humor

Ikeda: My own mentor Josei Toda used to enjoy telling me of once hearing Albert Einstein deliver a lecture. Aged twenty-nine at the time and deeply interested in mathematics, physics, and chemistry, Toda was very excited to hear that Einstein was coming to Japan. He later told me that the five-hour lecture on the special and general theories of relativity had been as moving as great art to him. Of course, as a Nobel laureate for physics, Einstein was a famous and respected figure. But Josei Toda was less impressed by his celebrity than by the personality revealed in the famous scientist's words and gestures. On one occasion, Toda referred to the lecture as a source of happiness that had lasted all his life. How did Albert Einstein impress you?

Pauling: I first met him in 1927 but became better acquainted with him in about 1932 at the California Institute of Technology. Later, when he was at Princeton, I was asked to join the Einstein Emergency Committee of Atomic Scientists. He allowed the vice-chairman to run the meetings and did not attend them himself. But he always requested my wife and me to visit and talk with him. We were the only ones. During our stay at Princeton, we discussed, not science, but mainly world affairs for about an hour every evening. We came to know him quite well. I think he liked my wife especially. They both had excellent senses of humor. When anything funny about national leaders and their behavior—or about anything else for that matter—was said, he would laugh uproariously.

Ikeda: In November, 1922, on his first visit to Japan, the government and people afforded Einstein a welcome of unprecedented warmth. In spite of the difficult content they represent, words like *theory of relativity* were on virtually all lips. Journalists were so taken with the famous scientist's scope, geniality, and modesty that they referred to him as "gentle as a smiling spring." One Japanese physicist, and poet, was so overjoyed that he said

Einstein has made it possible for
Human thought to mount the steepest stairs.
Our Einstein has brought the vastness
Of the Universe within our ken.
How numerous are the things he has given us!

In addition to his brilliance, as you say, he was a man of lively humor and an ardent pacifist. No doubt you can recall instances of his speaking to you about peace.

Pauling: Yes, many. I published an account of one such episode. Once in a discussion he said he felt he might have made a mistake in signing a letter to President Roosevelt recommending production of atomic bombs. He went on to say that perhaps he could be excused because he and his colleagues feared the Germans were working on the problem and would become masters of the world if they came up with a bomb first.

Immediately after saying goodbye to Einstein on that day, I took out my diary and wrote down precisely what he had said to me and the way he had said it. To an extent, he worried about his part in developing the atomic bomb. His theory of the relation between mass and energy was, of course, the basis for the bomb. His famous equation $E = mc^2$ (Energy equals mass times the square of the speed of light.) showed scientists that, if they could accelerate nuclear reactions, the atomic bomb would be feasible.

Ikeda: The knowledge that this was true must have put him in a very difficult situation. After World War II, certain Japanese acquaintances of his expressed doubt on this point. Einstein's reply to them suggests the bitter dilemma of conscience he was experiencing:

I am a dedicated (*entschiedener*) but not an *absolute* pacifist; this means that I am opposed to the use of force under any circumstances, except when confronted by an enemy who pursued the destruction of life as an *end in itself.* I have always condemned the use of the atomic bomb against Japan. However, I was completely powerless to prevent the fateful decision for which I am as little responsible as you are for the deeds of the Japanese in Korea and China. I have never said I would have approved the use of the atomic bomb against the Germans. I did believe that we had to avoid the contingency of Germany under Hitler being in *sole* possession of this weapon.

—*Einstein on Peace*

It is said that, upon hearing of the atomic bombing of Hiroshima, Einstein uttered only a brief expression of concentrated sorrow, *"Oh Weh!"*

As Heisenberg points out in his memoirs, other great scientists too were horrified to see the catastrophic outcome of some of their most brilliant work. He and his colleagues were in internment when they received news of the bombing of Hiroshima on August 6, 1945.

> Worst hit of all was Otto Hahn. Uranium fission, his most important scientific discovery, had been the crucial step on the road toward atomic power. And this step had now led to the horrible destruction of a large city and its population, of a host of unarmed and mostly innocent people. Hahn withdrew to his room, visibly shaken and deeply disturbed, and all of us were afraid that he might do himself some injury.

—Werner K. Heisenberg, *Physics and Beyond*

Like Hahn, Einstein was grief-stricken to learn of the tragedy. And perhaps his grief at this tragedy inspired him to become a noble standard-bearer in the postwar peace movement.

Pauling: Perhaps my own work for world peace would not have been very effective if I had not been invited to become a member of the board of trustees of the Emergency Committee of Atomic Scientists. As I have noted, Einstein was chairman of that committee and probably was responsible for my having been asked to join it. Before then, I had made some public talks about nuclear weapons and nuclear war; but it was Einstein's example that inspired my wife and me to devote energy and effort to pacifist activities.

Ikeda: Albert Einstein once said,

> . . .everyone who is seriously involved in the pursuit of science becomes convinced that a spirit is manifest in the laws of the Universe—a spirit vastly superior to that of man, and one in the face of which we with our modest powers must feel humble.

—Albert Einstein, *The Human Side—*
New Glimpses from His Archives

The harm attributed to runaway modern scientific technology—
especially the irreparable damage done to the natural environment
—arises because too many people have forgotten the humility Einstein
felt before what he called a "spirit."

Pauling: My wife and I talked with Albert Einstein many times,
and it is my opinion that he thought about the world much the way
that I did then and still do. The remark you quote can be misinterpreted
to suggest that Einstein believed in a supreme being. His statements
to us and some of his published comments seem to me to indicate that,
in this passage, he is referring to nature, to the universe, which continues to surprise scientists as more and more astonishing discoveries
are made about it.

Ikeda: During his youth, Einstein remarked that, whereas he
believed in the god postulated by Spinoza, that is, a god manifest in
the harmony of all being, he did not believe in a god that intervenes
in human fate and actions. In other words, he clearly did not accept
an anthropomorphic "supreme being" governing human destiny and
acting as a judge. Spinoza's god is an internal cause within all phenomena. Belief in it is a religious emotion oriented toward god as
nature or the governing principle of the universe.

In his *Out of My Later Years,* Einstein said, "Mere thinking cannot
give us a sense of the ultimate and fundamental ends. To make clear
these fundamental ends and valuations, and to set them fast in the
emotional life of the individual, seems to me precisely the most important function which religion has to perform in the social life of man."

In describing Einstein's appearance, Max Picard said that, unlike
those of many physicists, his face was not standardized. Any deliberate
attempts on his part to prevent his face from fitting into a given pattern
would have produced comical results. He made no such attempts. His
face had the simple, beautiful expression of an intellectual of an ex-
traordinarily cheerful character. Like his face, his personality fits no
standardized pattern. He was the kind of individual referred to in the
Buddhist doctrine according to which the universe is the individual
self and the individual self is the universe. Incidentally, I am pleased

that, like Spinoza, Einstein demonstrated a strong affinity for Buddhist ways of thinking in his late years. How would you characterize Albert Einstein and his achievements as scientist and champion of peace?

Pauling: I consider Albert Einstein, Isaac Newton, and Charles Darwin to be the three greatest scientists who have ever lived. Einstein made two very great contributions to science: the formulation of the special theory of relativity and later the formulation of the general theory of relativity. In addition, he made many other contributions, including recognition of the existence of photons and the explanation of the photoelectric effect. He was one of the greatest workers for world peace of his generation and deserved to receive a Nobel Peace Prize.

Ikeda: The world is in need of more people to carry on in the tradition of Einstein the man of peace. After the end of World War II, he insisted on the importance of limiting the powers of nationalist states, establishing a world federation, and creating global order. His ideas were frustrated, however, by the bipolar structure evolving from relations between the Soviet Union and the United States. Today, as the bipolar structure crumbles, the time has come to advance with renewed vigor the ideas Einstein cherished.

Before we leave this topic, what impressed you most in your own associations with Einstein?

Pauling: His reasonableness and his remarkable sense of humor impressed me most in his association with me and my wife.

When Are There Too Many Hydrogen Bombs?

Ikeda: On January 17, 1961, just as he was about to leave office, President Dwight D. Eisenhower said that a new, vast, and perilous force was threatening American democracy: the military-industrial complex.

Today that complex includes university and research scholars and has grown into the major support of the arms race. What are your thoughts on scientists who, as part of the system, have been responsible for research on and development of new weapons?

Pauling: For the past forty or forty-five years, I have lectured and written about this issue. From time to time, it has been suggested that scientists ought to refuse to work on the development and building of armaments. Since I believe in democracy, I prefer to see no single group—not even scientists—running the world. Scientists have an obligation to help their fellow citizens understand what the problems are but must not form a controlling oligarchy. Decisions must be made by the people as a whole.

I do not criticize scientists who, when looking for chances to apply their training and abilities, accept positions with, for instance, the Atomic Energy Commission or projects developing explosives for the military. During World War II, although I did some work on such military medical problems as treating the injured, much of my time was spent working on explosives. At the time, I saw no hope of ridding the world of war. I changed my views only after the development of the atomic bomb.

In short, I cannot criticize individuals for accepting jobs related to military development, as long as their work permits them to put their training and talents to use. Still, I admire those who refuse to do so. Members of an organization called the Society for Social Responsibility were supposed to refuse such work, and most of them did so.

Ikeda: The deeply involved specialist often cannot see the forest for the trees. The scientist becomes so concerned with individual fields that he loses sight of humanity and society as a whole. When this happens, mere means can be mistaken for goals. Nuclear weapons symbolize the way in which scientific technology can become estranged from humanity and its best interests.

The world is in dire need of specialists who are first and foremost knowing, discerning human beings. Harold Willens, an outstanding worker for peace from the United States, has said,

> It is nonsense to insist that resolving the nuclear arms dilemma should be left to the experts. The experts are, after all, the ones who created the policy that brought us to the present point of potentially terminal peril. The myth of expertise is exactly that—a myth. It takes scientific skills to make a hydrogen bomb. It takes only common sense to know when there are too many hydrogen bombs. And common sense is what is needed now.
>
> —Harold Willens, *The Trimtab Factor*

Your faith in democracy is, I believe, rooted in this kind of wholesome common sense. The essence of the problem is the relation between development in science and in the human spirit.

Science has brought us material blessings, but excessive faith in it has created problems by upsetting the balance in the human spiritual world. We have reached the point where we must employ scientific thinking and all our other faculties to combine spiritual enrichment and material well-being.

Pauling: I should prefer to reinterpret the issue as the relation between the advancement of science and the development of ethical and moral principles. The basic ethical principle on which science rests is the search for truth—the recognition of our ability to strive to determine what truth is. Young scientists are taught this, and all scientists must accept it.

The case of the politician is different. From time to time, I have said I should like to see the Congress of the United States pass even one piece of legislation on the basis of moral imperative alone. The usual arguments given for legislation have to do only with the advantages—not even of the whole world—but solely of the United States. For instance, it is considered a good thing to help starving people in other countries in order to strengthen their ability to buy the goods we have to sell them. We would make a great forward stride if we acted on the basis of the fundamental scientific principle of seeking the truth and the fundamental moral principle of minimizing human suffering.

Ikeda: In his late years, Albert Einstein concerned himself with the relation between knowledge—that is, objective truth—and ideals and right actions. He said,

> One can have the clearest and most complete knowledge of what *is*, and yet not be able to deduct from that what should be the *goal* of our human aspirations. Objective knowledge provides us with powerful instruments for the achievements of certain ends, but the ultimate goal itself and the longing to reach it must come from another source.

> —Albert Einstein, *Out of My Later Years*

We may set aside whatever Einstein may have meant by "another goal." But, if it could be oriented toward politics and the world of ideas and actions, objective scientific truth could help cultivate a truly global humanism—universalism—leading to the ultimate goal of lasting peace. Such a global view is essential if we are to overcome the narrow nationalist egoism that gravely hinders the attainment of world peace.

Renaissance People

Ikeda: When overspecialized in separate fields of expertise, scientists and technicians may find it difficult to understand other fields correctly and to locate their own endeavors accurately in the overall picture. This makes it hard for science and technology to develop in ways that truly benefit humanity. Do you consider this a problem? If so, do you see a way out of the dilemma?

Pauling: Certainly a specialist needs general knowledge, which, however, often requires great effort to acquire. For example, chemists have produced and investigated more than ten million chemical compounds—far too many for anyone to familiarize himself with in a lifetime. Fortunately, during my own life, chemical theory had expanded to such an extent that a chemist has no need to acquire this vast amount of information. He can obtain a good understanding of chemistry from an understanding of the principles determining the structures and properties of organic and inorganic compounds. A person who wants a good understanding of physics—a more basic subject than chemistry—must grasp enough general knowledge to know about electromagnetic waves, magnetism in general, physical properties, and mass-energy relations. But it is possible to have a sound overall understanding of physics without knowing such technical details as precisely how to measure superconductivity.

In the field of biology, with its more than ten million recognized species of animals and plants, it is obviously impossible to be a specialist in everything. A person interested in the taxonomy of the Coleoptera knows a great deal about beetles but may know much less about butterflies. Nonetheless, he probably has a general understanding of the nature of life in all its manifestations.

Although it is moving ahead rapidly and has reached the state where some of its basic principles are known, molecular biology has not yet been sufficiently unified for anyone to claim to understand it in relation to living organisms. But this level of knowledge will probably be reached soon.

There will always be people who acquire enough detailed experience of physics, mathematics, chemistry, biology, and other sciences to be called Renaissance people. They may not know everything in complete detail, but they have an understanding of everything.

On the other hand, people who do not want to exert the effort needed to acquire broad knowledge become specialists in, for instance, the measurement of superconductivity and properties of metals and alloys.

I do not consider this a serious dilemma. It has been said that perhaps no one else has as broad an understanding of sciences as I do. And there are not many. Most scientists are limited in their understanding. But many others try to find out more by reading scientific journalism. (Japanese scientists do this.) And I read such journals as the *Scientific American* to find out what is happening in cosmology and astronomy and to learn about new discoveries in physics, chemistry, and biology.

Ikeda: True Renaissance people with wide ranges of knowledge and vision are greatly needed.

Undeniably modern science has made startling contributions to humanity by helping reduce hunger and dealing with illness. Nonetheless, we must not optimistically allow an already hypertrophic and highly compartmentalized scientific-technological civilization to continue flying like a kite out of control. I suspect Einstein was troubled by concern for this kind of thinking in his late years, when he is reported to have said

> If I were a young man again and had to decide how to make a living, I would not try to become a scientist or scholar or teacher. I would rather choose to be a plumber or a peddler, in the hope of finding that modest degree of independence still available under present circumstances.
>
> —*Einstein on Peace*

In a letter to Louis de Broglie, Einstein described himself as an Australian ostrich. Not wanting to see quanta, he said he had thought to hide, ostrich fashion, by thrusting his head in the sands of relativism. You knew him well. No doubt his celebrated sense of humor is at work in this statement. But I think I am correct in sensing in it an underlying tone of sadness and pessimism.

Still Behaving Like Wolves

Ikeda: In your book *General Chemistry*, you say

Technical progress represents one way in which the world can be improved through science. Another way is through the social progress that results from application of the scientific method—through the development of "moral science."

Pauling: I wrote *General Chemistry*, which actually deals with college chemistry, in 1957 and began it with a quotation from Benjamin Franklin, who, two hundred years ago, said that science was progressing very rapidly and that he wished he could live longer because, in a hundred or a thousand years, scientific knowledge would be immense. He added that improvement in moral sciences would make men cease behaving like wolves to each other so that they would finally learn the meaning of what is now mistakenly called "humanity." At about this time, I formulated a scientific derivation of the basic moral principle of human behavior and considered it a good thing to mention it in my book on chemistry. To the best of my recollection, it is the only place in the book in which I discuss morality.

Ikeda: I am afraid Franklin would be very disappointed to learn that men continue to behave like wolves toward each other. In his late years, Hideki Yukawa delivered a simple, but meaningful, speech to an assembly of physicians. In it he said that, as he grew older, though he concentrated on research on physics and the exterior world, he became increasingly interested in his own inner nature and meaning. Studying the exterior world and investigating the self need not be different kinds of endeavors. He added

We live, not alone, but together with others. Those around us are, not isolated from, but connected with us in various ways. . . . I become increasingly convinced that love is the strongest connection. . . . at least, I hope that contacts with me will not be unpleasant and that I can make other people happy.

The sentiments expressed in this simple statement reflect the mellow understanding of age and the spirit of love and compassion embodied in higher religions and related to what you refer to as moral sciences.

Major Threats

Ikeda: Latest estimates claim that the population of the planet will grow to six billion by the end of this century. Few issues are debated more widely with fewer tangible results than the population explosion. What do you consider an ideal population for the Earth? What are your basic ideas about the population problem?

Pauling: The goal we should strive to achieve is a world population of a size permitting each individual to lead a good life—adequate food, clothing, and housing—and opportunities of contributing to the work of the world. As I have already said, everyone should have the kind of education that suits his needs and abilities. Moreover, everyone should have leisure and opportunities to travel and enjoy the wonders of the world.

I once wrote a book on this subject. At the time, the population of India had reached five hundred million. I recommended one hundred million as a goal population for India and urged the Indians to make the efforts required to achieve it. In addition, I recommended that the United States strive to decrease its population to one hundred and fifty million and that other nations make similar efforts to approach the ideal.

Ikeda: In dealing with the population of any given nation, we must attempt to ensure equally satisfactory standards of living for all people. Food, housing, education, welfare, health, and safety must be considered simultaneously on both the global and national levels.

As international relations expand and intensify, transport of essential products and intercourse among peoples will grow more frequent. Consequently, regional independence and global solidarity will become increasingly necessary. Peoples and nations must draw closer together and assist each other to attain the living standards you describe.

In addition, oneness with the environment is of the greatest significance. The minds of people divorced from nature grow desolate and arid. Citizens of industrialized nations are the ones who often have least associations with nature and the comfort and peace contact with it brings.

At present, human activities all over the planet wreak havoc on the ecological system by felling forests, farming in ways that stimulate desertification, and upsetting meteorological conditions by dumping huge quantities of carbon dioxide into the atmosphere. Of course, questions of energy and natural resources are involved in this process too. But we must constantly attempt to understand the nature of the ecological system in which we live and strive to keep our population within the limits of the system's abilities to restore itself.

Pauling: I foresee two serious problems demanding solutions in the twenty-first century. One is limiting world population. The other is eliminating war. The existence of nuclear weapons prevents the great nuclear powers from going to war with one another. Nevertheless, wars persist, mostly among smaller countries. The great nations must begin utilizing their powers to help achieve solutions to the problems now causing war and taking tremendous tolls in human suffering.

Ikeda: About ten years ago, an article in the *Observer* made the interesting statement that mankind faces six major threats: the population explosion, food shortages, exhaustion of natural resources, environmental pollution, misuse of nuclear power, and technology run wild. All are global problems the solutions to which demand measures transcending the framework of the national state. But progress in their solution is still unsatisfactory because of the emergence of a seventh threat in the form of an obstructing force of two aspects: human moral delusion and prevalent abuses within national political structures.

As a Buddhist, I feel that special attention must be paid to moral delusion. An oriental proverb says, "It is easier to defeat the traitor in the mountains than the traitor in the heart." Because he is invisible, a traitor in the heart is a formidable foe. This is why, while combating external threats like war, environmental pollution, and the population explosion, we must wage fierce battle with this internal threat as well.

We are now only a little more than a decade away from the twenty-first century, which I should like to envision in terms of a century of life. As a scientist, how do you envision the coming age?

The Century of Life

Pauling: I assume that by a "century of life" you mean a century in which greater attention will be paid to human beings and their happiness and health. I might characterize the twenty-first century as a time in which molecular biology will flourish and we shall obtain a greater understanding of the nature of life than we have now. In this sense, I too think it is a good idea to regard the twenty-first century as a century of life.

Ikeda: The century of life must be a time that manifests greater respect for human life and affords greater opportunities for happiness. To prepare for the advent of such an age we require deeper understanding of the nature of life itself. Further we must create a human society consonant with the new knowledge we obtain about life. Understanding of life may be acquired from various aspects and by means of diverse methodologies. Molecular biology, the study of the molecules of which living things are constituted, deals with proteins, enzymes, carbohydrates, fats, and nucleic acids. This field of research has made astonishing contributions to our comprehension of the physical facets of life. In the coming century, the detailed information molecular-biological study will provide about life forms will no doubt greatly influence such fields as medicine and genetic engineering.

But above and beyond the physical aspects, improved understanding of life's spiritual aspects would be extremely promising. In the

West, the depth psychology of Freud and Adler plumbed the innermost mind. The great Buddhist scholar Vasubandhu, who lived in the fourth and fifth centuries, systematized the internal human spirit in a philosophical structure called *Yogachara,* "Consciousness Only," which became the foundation of one of the major branches of Mahayana Buddhism.

Whereas Freud and his followers investigated the subconscious, Vasubandhu actually provided the subconscious—what Arnold J. Toynbee called the psychological universe—with a theoretical order.

According to the Consciousness Only interpretation, the *Manas* consciousness is the subconscious foundation of the conscious self. It is created by a flow of life known as the *Alaya* consciousness, in which latent energy (called seeds) for all physical and psychological functions are stored. Cause-and-effect relations within the *Alaya* consciousness determine the operations of the *Manas* consciousness and of all other levels of consciousness. I believe a modern intellectual investigation of this venerable Buddhist psychological system could make great contributions to an understanding of the true nature of life. A combined Science of Life representing cooperative mutual study and interchange between molecular biology, in the physical realm, and research into the innermost mind, in the spiritual realm, might promise brilliant results in the name of the coming century of life.

Orthomolecular Medicine

Ikeda: Although their number is not great, some doctors in the United States today practice what is called orthomolecular medicine, a term that I believe you originated. What are some of the characteristics of orthomolecular medicine? Why were you motivated to undertake the study of this field?

Pauling: Orthomolecular medicine—yes, the word is my coinage—means achieving and maintaining optimum health by means of establishing and maintaining optimum concentrations of essential molecules, like those of ascorbic acid. It is better to treat disease by means of substances occurring normally in the body than to resort to powerful synthetic substances that generally produce toxic side effects. By *orthomolecular medicine,* I mean therapy entailing varying concentrations of such low-toxicity substances as vitamin C and other vitamins, which are normally found in the body and which are necessary to good health. Apart from the use of vitamins, treatment of diabetes mellitus with insulin is a good example of orthomolecular medicine.

Hereditary diabetes mellitus results in insufficient production of the pancreatic hormone insulin. Insulin stimulates increased extraction of glucose from the bloodstream into the cells, where it can be metabolized. Without sufficient insulin, glucose concentrations in the blood become abnormally high, resulting in the various symptoms of the disease. Insulin extracted from the pancreases of cattle or pigs is molecularly very similar to human insulin and acts physiologically in virtually the same way. The orthomolecular procedure of injecting such insulin into the patient permits normal glucose metabolism.

Other orthomolecular ways of combating diabetes mellitus include restriction of amounts of sugar ingested and increased intakes of vitamin C to reduce the need for insulin. Unlike vitamin C, oral insulin is a synthetic drug foreign to the human body. Its use is not orthomolecular and can have undesirable side effects.

Ikeda: What was the immediate stimulus inspiring you to turn your attention to this field?

Pauling: As I have said, I like to understand the universe. I became involved in orthomolecular medicine when I discovered something I did not understand and wanted to understand. When I learned that, in Saskatchewan, Canada, Dr. Abram Hoffer and Dr. Humphry Osmond were giving vitamins to schizophrenic patients, I was astonished to notice the vast amounts of the vitamin it is possible to take without harmful effects of any kind.

Ikeda: We all know that vitamins are important to health, but when did people in general first become what might be called vitamin-conscious?

Pauling: It had to do with a disease called scurvy, which has been known for centuries, although clear understanding of the disorder as dietary in nature was not forthcoming until 1911.

Initially characterized by weakness, depression, restlessness, and fatigue, scurvy rapidly leads to ulcerated gums, loss of teeth, bad breath, intramuscular bleeding, diarrhea, pulmonary and renal failure, and ultimately death.

Its worse ravages were confined to sailors and others who, for logistic or other reasons, were kept for protracted periods on diets of biscuit and salt meat—in other words, diets very low in vitamin C.

Prevention of scurvy through proper diet came about only very slowly and gradually. In the eighteenth century, the famous English explorer Captain James Cook (1728–1779) had remarkable success in controlling the sickness by ensuring that the men on his ships ate such foods as sauerkraut, wild vegetables, and a drink called spruce beer made from spruce needles. Thanks to the use of these antiscorbutic agents, not a single one of Cook's men died of scurvy during his three celebrated voyages to the Pacific, although the disease was taking terrific tolls among the crews of other long-voyage vessels in the same period.

Since the time of the sixteenth-century English admiral Sir John Hawkins, it had been understood that citrus fruit—lemons, oranges, and limes—were a good addition to the seaman's diet for the sake of preventing scurvy. The juices of these fruits are rich in ascorbic acid (vitamin C). And, in the late eighteenth century, after the nutritional value of citrus fruits had been recognized, the British Admiralty ordered a daily ration of fresh lime juice for all sailors, with the result that scurvy disappeared from the British navy.

The word *vitamin* evolved from *vitamine* (composed of the Latin *vita* and *amine*, compounds of nitrogen including the amino acids. The Polish biochemist Casimir Funk, who coined the word, developed a theory of vitamines in which he suggested that there are four substances commonly found in ordinary foods and important in protecting from beriberi, scurvy, pellagra, and rickets. Since it was later discovered that some of these substances actually contain no nitrogen the word was changed to *vitamin*.

Still later, an American scientist named E. V. McCollum divided vitamins into fat-soluble A, water-soluble B, and water-soluble C categories. In the early part of the twentieth century, a Hungarian scientist named Albert Szent-Gyorgyi isolated pure vitamin C. He and a colleague, an English sugar chemist named W. M. Haworth named it ascorbic acid, or the acid that acts against scurvy.

The ascorbic acid molecule is very simple and may be manufactured from glucose, the major fuel cells use to sustain life. These very facts suggest the importance of vitamin C and help explain why it is found throughout the tissues of the body.

Ikeda: As you illustrate with the history of the elimination of scurvy from the British navy, vitamins are extremely important to good health. You call them low-toxic. Does this mean they produce no harmful side effects at all?

Pauling: Drugs are toxic. For instance, the more a person takes of the pain-killer aspirin, the more effective the drug. But massive doses of aspirin are fatal. It is possible to take fifteen or twenty a day without ill effect, but three or four times those amounts would kill. Doctors prescribe the largest possible doses of drugs within the limits of toxicity.

Vitamin C is a very powerful substance. A small pinch is enough to protect from death from scurvy. But it is possible to take great amounts of vitamin C with total safety. From reading Hoffer and Osmond, I learned that one may take a thousand, five thousand, or even ten thousand times the one pinch of vitamin C without risking fatality. Several vitamins have practically no toxicity. I became interested to know how much of other vitamins a person should take, not merely to prevent mortal illness, but also to remain in optimum health.

For an animal to remain in the best possible health, many different kinds of molecules must be present in the body. Some living organisms can synthesize what they need. Others are less capable in this respect.

For example, the red bread mold (Neurospora) can synthesize everything it needs, provided it has water, inorganic salts, an inorganic source of nitrogen, a source of carbon, and a single vitamin called biotin. It has employed its internal biochemical mechanisms to synthesize whatever else it has required to survive for hundreds of millions of years.

Ikeda: How capable at synthesizing are more complex organisms?

Pauling: Much less. In the distant past, as they came to eat foods supplying them with the vitamins they needed, through mutations, many animals lost the ability to synthesize these substances on their own. For instance, tests have suggested that the ability to synthesize ascorbic acid (vitamin C) was lost in a common ancestor of the primates. This is why today human beings, the rhesus monkey, the Formosan long-tail monkey, and other primates cannot produce their own vitamin C but must ingest it as a supplement.

Mutations robbing organisms of the capability to synthesize enzymes are not uncommon. Possibly, at some distant time, when the precursor of the primates was living somewhere with plenty of the kinds of foods that supply vitamin C, a mutagenic agent affected it, rendering it incapable of synthesizing ascorbic acid. Some of the offspring of the mutated animals would inherit the incapacity. But, since it lightened their bodies' load of synthesizing labor and since they had plenty of food to supply the vitamin they could no longer produce, the loss turned out to be an advantage. And, as laws of evolution show, mutant creatures with an advantage of this kind survive and gradually replace earlier strains.

Most animals need no ascorbic acid to supplement their diet because they make it in their own cells. But human beings are different; they cannot make it, but have to get it from their food or from vitamin C tablets.

Ikeda: I know you recommend taking vitamins in massive doses. Why do you think this is a good idea?

Pauling: I believe that, sooner or later, it will be possible to cure many different diseases by means of the branch of orthomolecular medicine called megavitamin therapy. Ample evidence indicates that large doses of vitamin C can control a wide range of illnesses including the common cold, influenza, hepatitis, and even such conditions as schizophrenia, cardiovascular disease, and cancer.

The reason for this is easy to understand. As I have said, drugs are powerful substances that often produce undesirable side effects. Vitamin C, on the other hand, is natural to the body and plays an essential part in all the body's biochemical reactions and protective mechanisms. With traditionally recommended intakes of vitamin C, these reactions and mechanisms fail to operate efficiently. The optimum intake of vitamin C, which is much larger than traditional doses, makes for really good—not the generally accepted moderately poor—health and offers intensified protection against illness.

Ikeda: Do you mean that it has a salutary effect on the immune system? Could this have significance for dealing with AIDS?

Pauling: A great deal of evidence leads us to believe that vitamin C is indispensable to the efficient working of the immune system, since it is involved in the synthesis of many of the antibody molecules and the production of functioning cells that destroy antigenic molecules or cells.

In a study published in 1984, Dr. Robert F. Cathcart stated that limited observations of patients given large doses of ascorbic acid led him to believe that vitamin C suppresses the symptoms of AIDS and can reduce the incidence of secondary infection. Of course, much more research is needed on this topic.

Like many other people, I have been astonished to see the value of vitamin C in treating virtually all diseases. It is possible for this single substance to exert diverse and far-reaching beneficial influence because it is involved in many biochemical reactions that strengthen the natural defense mechanisms of the human body. We can triumph over disease only when our body fluids and organs contain enough vitamin C to achieve the goal. The doses we must take, however, are obviously far bigger than what medical and nutritional authorities recommend.

I have been fascinated by the vitamin question for twenty years and have spent a large part of my time trying to discover optimum vitamin dosages. No one knows the limits of vitamin-dose sizes, but clearly they can be very large. For instance, I knew a man who took an eighth of a kilogram of vitamin C daily to control a cancer. His dose was about one hundred thousand times as large as the one required to protect from scurvy.

Owing to a factor called biochemical individuality, which means each person has different nutritional and chemical needs, it is difficult to determine the optimum dosage of vitamin C. Studies have shown—and I accept their conclusion—that optimum intake of ascorbic acid for human beings may extend over a very wide range (250 milligrams to 20 grams a day). Nonetheless, I estimate that the proper use of this and other vitamin supplements could extend the period of well-being and length of life for most people by from twenty-five to thirty-five years. I am pleased to know that my own work in this field may help improve the health of every person on earth.

Ikeda: In the Orient, medical practice is referred to as the benevolent art. Your work on orthomolecular medicine certainly deserves this description. Your approach to it reflects the compassionate attitude of the Bodhisattvas, whose helpful philosophy is the heart of the spirit of practicing Buddhism. In the Buddhist context, compassion means relieving pain and giving happiness. In the excessively profit-oriented modern world, the mere desire to extend such compassion is admirable. How much more precious is actual work towards the accomplishment of the altruistic goal. Your pioneering efforts in orthomolecular medicine transcend intellectual curiosity to enter the realm of compassionate caring.

Pauling: In addition to wanting to answer a question, I hoped to relieve suffering caused by poor health. Similarly, in my work for peace, I have tried to alleviate the suffering caused—today, as in the past—by war.

I became interested in biology and medicine at twenty-eight years of age, when a division of the biological sciences was established at the California Institute of Technology. Thomas Hunt Morgan was chairman, and there were many able biologists on the staff.

For many years I sought out biological and medical problems to the solutions of which I might be able to contribute. I worked on the structure of hemoglobin and on protein structures in general. With my associates and students, I carried out many studies in the field of immunology. This work led us to recognize that sickle-cell anemia is a molecular disease and that many other diseases too can be classified as molecular in nature. As I have pointed out, the body requires the presence of certain molecules for good health. One of them is the ascorbic-acid molecule, or vitamin C.

In 1970, realizing that the medical profession ignores the large amounts of scientific and medical evidence for the value of massive intakes of vitamin C, I decided to write a book on the topic: *Vitamin C and the Common Cold,* published in 1970. Two years earlier, I had written a paper, which was published in *Science,* on orthomolecular psychiatry. This paper was essentially about the value of nutrients in relation to mental health.

Doctors Humphry Osmond and Abram Hoffer of the Saskatchewan Hospital, in Canada—whom I already mentioned—have done outstanding work in this connection. With their colleagues, they have shown that orthomolecular treatment entailing supplements of niacin and vitamin C, plus other nutrients, is a very valuable adjunct to conventional therapy for schizophrenia.

At the present, there are many orthomolecular psychiatrists. I am glad that progress is being made in stimulating understanding of the importance of improved nutrition in the treatment of mental disorders. Nonetheless, although used in some psychiatric hospitals, orthomolecular medicine is still not generally accepted as a treatment for schizophrenia. The American medical profession remains reluctant to accept its validity, in spite of the abundant evidence to support it.

Ikeda: Do you consider this a major shortcoming of contemporary medicine?

Pauling: Yes. The greatest defect of medicine today is the bias physicians have against the proper use of vitamins and other orthomolecular substances in the preservation of health and treatment of disease. Physicians may justly be conservative in their practices; but, if progress is to be made, the medical profession as a whole must be open to new ideas. It is not, however. For example, fifty years ago, Claus W. Jungeblut first showed that ascorbic acid can inactivate certain viruses, thus providing protection against some viral diseases. But the medical profession in general gave his idea so poor a reception that he became discouraged and went into another field of medicine.

Ikeda: How would you describe the ideal approach for the medical profession to adopt?

Pauling: Accepting the value of preventing disease instead of merely treating it after a crisis has arisen.

Ikeda: I agree entirely. Medical science does seem to be moving in the direction of emphasizing prevention largely because of a change in the nature of prevailing illnesses. The most serious sicknesses facing contemporary humanity—cancer, cardiovascular illness, diabetes, and so on—are of such a nature that, if allowed to progress beyond a certain point, they become extremely difficult to arrest and cure. Naturally, in dealing with them, stress must be placed on preventing their emergence or curing them at an early stage. This is why I agree with you that the preservation of health is of primary concern now and will grow even more important in the years to come. A sickly child myself, I derived considerable knowledge of illness from extensive reading and from my own experience. This reinforces my agreement with what you say.

As in the case of illness, we do very well indeed to concentrate on preventing the pathological condition known as war instead of merely coping with it once it has broken out.

Do you have a special regimen that helps you stay healthy and prevent sickness?

Pauling: My health remains good because I have never smoked cigarettes or used tobacco or any similar substance to any extent and because I have improved my nutrition in the ways described in my book *How to Live Longer and Feel Better*.

Prescribing very restrictive and ascetic diets and health regimens produces very little in the way of results because people usually find them too hard to adhere to or too much of a nuisance. That is why I recommend that people do not smoke; that they eat good food—not in quantities that will make them obese—and that they supplement their diets with vitamins, especially vitamin C, in massive doses.

Ikeda: We tend to become more concerned about health the older we grow. I used to smoke but have given it up. I shall certainly refer to your book to find ways to improve my nutrition, which is, of course, vital to good health. Although I cannot drink them, many people find alcoholic beverages pleasant and relaxing. What place do they have in your system for health and long life?

Pauling: I recommend that people not smoke tobacco and restrict themselves to a minimum of sugar (glucose). As far as alcohol is concerned, I recommend that people enjoy it, but only in moderation. A study conducted in California has shown that moderate drinkers tend to be healthier than teetotalers but that heavy drinkers—people who have more than four drinks a day—tend to be less healthy. Aside from this, I urge people to get a moderate amount of exercise regularly, sleep seven or eight hours a night, avoid stressful situations, work at an occupation they enjoy, and generally enjoy life.

Ikeda: The foundation of any health regimen should be good nutrition, exercise, adequate rest, and a regular daily rhythm. Effort to ensure this last is especially significant in busy modern society. Sound physical and mental health is the key to a creative, valuable life. If this is generally understood, why are so many people today no more than semi-healthy?

Pauling: It is true, that many people are not as healthy as they should and can be. What is referred to as ordinary good health is actually ordinary poor health because people usually are improperly nourished and fail to take orthomolecularly correct amounts of vitamins and other important substances. People who follow the nutritional advice in *How To Live Longer and Feel Better*, however, can enjoy longer, healthier lives and suffer much less from disease.

Ikeda: Rapid economic development, freedom from hunger, balanced diet, vigorous advances in medical science, and an established medical system help account for the longevity of the Japanese people— among the most long-lived in the world. Statistics show that reduction of the infant-mortality rate reflects strongly in longer average Japanese life spans.

In spite of this longevity, however, the people of Japan are not always healthy. They suffer from increasingly frequent physical and psychosomatic sicknesses, neuroses, and pathological psychological conditions that, though arrestable through therapy, tend to recur. Sometimes neuroses and psychosomatic symptoms can be alleviated to the extent that the sufferer seems perfectly well. Such people—the semi-healthy—suffer from many complaints and endure much anguish. It is to be hoped that the correct nutrition you advocate can contribute to the improvement of their condition.

Increases in the frequencies of psychologically caused illnesses indicate the need to reexamine contemporary lifestyles. This is all the more important since many apparently purely physical illnesses, like cancer and cardiac disease, are profoundly related to mental anxiety, despair, sorrow, and indifference to life. Obviously anxiety and sorrow affect neuroses and depression.

This suggests that sound spiritual health is essential to good physical condition. In the modern world, where human relations are often superficial and diversity of value criteria can threaten the foundations of even so venerable an institution as the family, maintaining good spiritual health is difficult. I believe that religion is a source of the kind of strength needed to cope with the contemporary human condition.

For instance, the very foundation of Buddhism is a system for dealing with the most basic kinds of suffering experienced by human kind: birth, aging, illness, and death. In helping us to deal with these fundamental experiences, Buddhism points the way to a path of mentally and physically sound self-realization and triumph over suffering.

How do you suggest that we might combat the stress and stressors responsible for the semi-healthy state in which so many members of modern society find themselves?

Stress

Pauling: We should strive to develop economic and political systems that decrease the amount of stress on the individual human being. A good way to do this is to abolish war.

A high intake of vitamin C has value in helping control the effects of stress. Dr. T. W. Anderson, a leading investigator at the University of Toronto Medical School, says that vitamin C might be called the anti-stress vitamin.

Ikeda: The many stress-causing factors to which we are subjected may be divided into environmental elements (heat, cold, noise, and so on); chemical elements; physiological elements (hunger, fatigue, infections); and psychological elements (fear, anger, and so on). When it strikes, war triggers all these kinds of stress factors. It brings on hunger, poverty, and sometimes epidemic. Obviously it makes people anxious and fearful. In this sense, you are quite right to say that abolishing war is an excellent way to decrease stress.

Vitamin C may well contribute greatly to stress reduction by raising physiological resistance to such stressors as environmental change. But this is not the entire picture. Stress can have an immense variety of sources: the oversophistication of modern society, the burden of official control exerted on the individual (especially onerous in Japan), frustrations in human relations, changing value criteria, an unwieldy plethora of information defying orderly treatment, the deterioration of traditional institutions like the family, and on and on. We must of course strive to compel governments and social organizations to do everything possible to reduce stress-causing situations. But we must also work to cultivate in each individual powers of mental and physical resistance to stress.

Some people are naturally more stress-resistant than others. As Professor Albert Bandura, a psychiatrist at Stanford University, has said self-confident people with a purpose in life resist stress better than the insecure and vacillating.

Still, when all is said and done, there can be no such thing as a stress-free life. In *The Mirage of Health*, the late American bacteriologist Rene Dubos, with whom I once had a very lively discussion, says that, whereas it is pleasant to imagine a world without worry and a life without stress or strain, this is only a dream of the lazy. Mr. Dubos goes on to say that human life is a dynamic process but that paradise is a static concept. It is folly to attempt to discover a separate paradise on Earth. Human beings have chosen to struggle, not necessarily for themselves, but for the sake of eternally advancing economic, intellectual, and ethical development.

I agree with Mr. Dubos's belief that meaning and mission in life arise from the struggle for self-realization and the perfection of human nature. Paradoxically, stress can be a stimulant in the noble struggle. In connection with putting stress to use for the betterment of humanity, religion has an important role to play.

Euthanasia

Ikeda: The pros and cons of euthanasia have been debated since the days of the ancient Greeks. The argument continues today under a somewhat novel guise. Over a decade ago, a group of doctors and other professional people stirred up considerable debate by actively advocating euthanasia. The focus of the movement has now shifted from mercy killing to prevent suffering to euthanasia for the sake of death with dignity. Cases of so-called assisted suicide have occurred in the United States and have even been taken to court. Probably advances in the medical therapy for the prolongation of life have resulted in this situation. What is your attitude toward people who insist on the human right to die and the right to die with dignity?

Pauling: The word *euthanasia* is subject to misinterpretation. I am most interested in the human being's right to die in dignity. I support efforts to restrain physicians who operate intensive-care clinics and strive to keep patients alive as long as possible merely to return them to consciousness after they are essentially dead. In some cases, a patient is brought back to awareness one day; and a crisis a day or a week later returns the person to the moribund condition. This process may be repeated over and over, although there is no hope of true recovery. Such a practice is wrong since it causes the dying patient unnecessary suffering.

A terminally ill patient has the right to die in dignity. I can see no reason to keep a brain-dead patient alive, perhaps year after year, by such techniques as intravenous feeding. In short, I oppose misusing modern medical technology to revive time and time again people for whom there is no hope of permanent recovery. Although I have not done it yet, I intend to write a statement to the effect that, if illness or injury puts me in a hopeless condition, I wish to be allowed to die, without unnecessary suffering, but with dignity. Once again, I apply my basic principle of minimizing human suffering.

Of course, efforts should be made to alleviate conditions. To reduce suffering, doctors give patients dying of cancer doses of pain-killing morphine that would be addictive under ordinary circumstances. But, when the case is truly hopeless, life-support systems and intravenous feeding should be discontinued.

On the other hand, protection from doctors is essential. For instance, we must not tolerate situations in which doctors allow patients to die out of personal reluctance to provide suitable treatment. Euthanasia demands careful formulation of and rigorous adherence to criteria.

Ikeda: As I have said, in the past, the euthanasia issue focused on pain, especially in instances of illnesses like terminal cancer involving such great suffering that the patient's life seemed hardly worth saving. Fairly recently, a certain Japanese physician delivered a fatal dose of a drug to relieve a terminally ill cancer patient of further suffering. But, with advances in medical treatment and the emergence of specialized pain clinics and hospices, reduction of pain has ceased to be the focal issue. Since I agree with you that minimizing suffering is of the greatest importance, I hope that pain clinics will make still further advances in the future.

Advances in medical therapy have resulted in instances in which artificial prolongation of life and the desire for death with dignity have become the center of the euthanasia debate. Brain death is one such instance. After a person has been diagnosed irrecoverably brain dead, doctors must decide whether to continue therapy or disconnect life-support systems.

At one time, Japanese physicians employed medication to keep the heart of a brain-dead patient alive for one hundred days. Without special therapy, the heart usually ceases to beat within from three days to a week after brain death. In cases of this kind, I believe life-support therapy should be suppressed. But the wishes of the patient himself— his own right of self-determination—deserve maximum respect.

To be capable of clearly stating his wishes on such a serious matter beforehand, a person must already have formulated a clear philosophy of life and death. Relatives and loved ones must demonstrate concern and must make all possible efforts to assist the patient to meet death with dignified composure. The physician must offer both them and the patient full, sympathetic support. When these preconditions are fulfilled, it is proper to determine the suitable level of therapy to afford the patient.

In Japan—as in China, Korea, and other parts of the Orient—the wishes of the family often exert great influence on decisions of this kind. This is not to say that the rights of the patient himself are considered negligible.

Consistent with your principles, you hold that suffering should be minimized and that the individual human being has the right to die with dignity. From the Buddhist standpoint, death with dignity entails coping with three kinds of suffering: physiological, psychological, and existential (that is, religious). Medical science and such institutions as pain clinics have the duty of dealing with physiological suffering. Hospices are achieving much in alleviating psychological suffering, which has tremendous impact on loved ones and friends as well as on the patient. The patient's own philosophy of life and death and his religious views must supply the strength to bring relief from the last of the three kinds of suffering.

A dignified death, in the Buddhist interpretation, is one in which these three kinds of suffering have been overcome, physical and mental tranquility has been attained, and the patient can regard the termination of life with a peaceful mind. Life-prolonging medical technology may be used to assist people in dying this way but must never be allowed to aggravate suffering.

Attitudes toward brain death have been well established for a long time in the West. In Japan, however, it remains a topic of heated debate. The level of Japanese diagnostic and organ-transplant technology is on a par with that of the West. But, although even now that transplant surgery has become relatively common, national traits and deep-rooted oriental ideas of life and death complicate discussions of brain death. What are your views on the subject?

Pauling: No one has ever recovered from the brain-dead state, during which measurable electrical brain waves cease to exist and electrodes produce only a level response. A person in such a state cannot be revived. If permission has been obtained, I consider it quite proper to allow such an individual to die and to use his organs for transplanting. No suffering is involved. A brain-dead person experiences no pain. And there is no reason to keep such a person alive.

Ikeda: The general population of Japan is just now beginning to realize fully that no one, as you say, can recover from the brain-dead state.

The process of determining brain death and acting on the decision goes through three phases. First, it is necessary to decide that brain death represents actual ultimate decease, after which no resuscitation is possible. It is then essential to establish standards for making such a judgment in individual cases and for deciding the certainty of judgments made on the basis of those standards. Third, once death has been acknowledged on the part of all concerned parties (including opinions of family members and written statements by the deceased, if any such statements exist), if consent is given to disconnect life-support systems, it must be decided whether to use the patient's organs for transplanting.

As you suggest, there is no problem about the first stage. Current Japanese criteria for determination of brain death are stricter than those used in the West. Nonetheless, some doctors have argued that patients declared brain dead on the basis of those standards have responded to other kinds of intensive examination. Probably, however, these doubts within the medical community will be resolved with the passing of time. When, after thorough examination, physicians have declared a patient brain dead on the basis of responsible standards established by the medical community, the individual has passed the line at which revival is possible. In Buddhist terms, the instant of death has passed.

Owing to profound connections with Japanese ethnic and general oriental views of life and death, the third phase of the process presents more serious problems. It is impossible to go into the issue thoroughly here; suffice it to say that Buddhists do not regard death as the reduction of human life to nothing. According to Buddhist philosophy, after the instant of death, life blends with the universe itself. All emotions experienced during life—joys and sorrows—fuse with the universal life-force as latent energies. Certainly, at death, consciousness fails; and the being enters the realm of the subconscious, the vast region in which Buddhism locates a great original self supporting all individual selves. In this realm, consciousness of the individual self fades. But the subconscious, original self remains active. Of course, no physical pain is involved at this stage. The original self is capable of experiencing tranquility and joy—conceivably, psychological and existential suffering too. On the basis of this philosophy of life and death, I insist that decisions about organ transplants must take into consideration the wishes of the dying party and his family.

The Japanese people have been slow to sanction organ transplants because of the combination of persisting Buddhist, indigenous Shinto, and Confucian principles constituting the traditional background of their attitudes toward the human body. These views hold that the spirit inhabits the corpse, with which it is united. On the basis of this belief, the Japanese hesitate to permit removal for transplant of organs from a person declared brain dead.

For such surgery to find general acceptance in Japan, public opinion must accept Western ideas. (I discuss these points in greater detail in a series of articles entitled "Brain Death.")

3

A World Free of War

The Death of Death

Ikeda: The atomic bombings of Hiroshima and Nagasaki, in August, 1945, ushered in the nuclear age, simultaneously invalidating all former interpretations of the nature of war. Because it has come to threaten the destruction of civilization itself and the annihilation of the human race, war can never again be regarded as what Clausewitz termed an extension of diplomatic or political means.

Pauling: The Hiroshima bomb descended from the B-29 by parachute and exploded over the central part of the city at a height of about 2,200 feet. Within a matter of seconds, many thousands of people were killed by falling buildings or by radiation from the fire-ball, which was hotter than the surface of the sun. It is estimated that, by 1950, about 300,000 people had died as a consequence of the bombings of Hiroshima and Nagasaki.

Weapons available now, of course, are much more powerful than those used against Japan at the end of World War II. Deaths from the use of even small nuclear bombs of the kinds currently at the disposal of several nations would certainly range in the millions, and the aftereffects of fallout and radiation would extend over hundreds of square kilometers. Undeniably, nuclear weapons have changed our world because they are a million times more destructive than any of the bombs used before their advent.

Ikeda: What was your initial emotion upon hearing news of the Hiroshima and Nagasaki tragedies?

Pauling: Within a short time of learning that nuclear weapons had been detonated over Hiroshima and Nagasaki, with tremendous suffering and loss of life, I came to the conclusion that the existence of such weapons compels us to abandon war as a means of settling disputes between and among nations. Up until that time, I had doubted that war could ever be eliminated.

Ikeda: Yes, the situation before Hiroshima and Nagasaki was entirely different from the situation prevailing after the bombings. The emergence of nuclear weapons was a fateful event.

The American journalist Jonathan Schell put this apocalpytic fatefulness succinctly when he said, "Extinction is more terrible—is the more radical nothingness—because extinction ends death just as surely as it ends birth and life. Death is only death; extinction is the death of death."

In a discussion we shared, Raul Alfonsin, the former president of Argentina, censured the nuclear arms race as deprivation of the human right to existence and as a self-contradictory attempt to apply traditional war standards to the nuclear age. This is why it has become impossible to overemphasize the importance of striving to create a world free of war.

Pauling: As I have said, until 1945, I doubted that the world would ever be rid of war and foresaw a third world conflict between the Soviet Union and the United States, or at any rate between communists and capitalists. In 1945, however, I came to think, as did Albert Einstein, that the existence of nuclear weapons had finally made it imperative to abandon war once and for all. As seemed only logical to me, these weapons force us to accept the idea of coexistence and cooperation. Now that the facts about nuclear weapons are relatively well known to the general public, we must realize that the future of the human race depends on our willingness and ability to cooperate and work together to solve global problems without belligerence.

World War II and After

Ikeda: A great change in approach is indeed essential if humanity is to survive. During World War II, many scientists were engaged in the development of the atomic bomb. What kind of work were you doing then?

Pauling: During World War II, I lived in Pasadena, California, where I continued my work as a professor at the California Institute of Technology. From 1939 to 1945, I carried on research for the National Defense Research Committee and was a member of that organization's Division 8, which approved contracts with various investigators in the explosives field.

As the responsible investigator for fourteen contracts, I worked mainly on problems at the request of the armed forces. At the end of the war, President Truman conferred upon me the Presidential Medal for Merit for my services during this period.

Ikeda: To what extent were you aware of the work of the Manhattan Project, which, initiated in 1942, carried out research on an explosive device based on nuclear fission and which ultimately produced the atomic bomb?

Pauling: I had some knowledge of the Manhattan Project. Robert Oppenheimer (1904–1967), who headed it, came to Pasadena and asked me to be in charge of the chemistry section at Los Alamos. He gave me only a limited amount of information. I declined the offer. Thereafter, although I received bits of further information from time to time, I was not kept well informed. And this did not disturb me. At the end of the war, I was satisfied to see that Hitler and his associates had been defeated in their attempt to conquer the world.

Ikeda: Experience of the war inspired you and me and many others to devote ourselves to the cause of peace. I was seventeen in

1945. Our family, like those of countless other people, had been ruined by the war. My older brother had been killed in Burma, and my own physical constitution had been weakened by forced labor in a munitions factory. My unrelenting hatred of war and total devotion to peace derive from these bitter experiences.

Pauling: Yes, many of us were inspired to speak out against war not long after the fighting had stopped. For instance, in 1945, within a month or two of the dropping of the atomic bombs, I began giving talks about nuclear weapons. I spoke to luncheon clubs, labor unions, student groups, and pacifist meetings about the catastrophe that would result from nuclear war and about the paramount importance of preserving the peace.

I knew the nature of these weapons. And I had no clearance problems because I had not been involved in the Manhattan Project. I believed I was free to talk and to make use of my recognized ability to explain scientific matters to laymen. Immediately after the bombings, I was asked time and time again to speak on nuclear weapons.

At first, I spoke only about physics and the nature of nuclear fission. Within a few months, however, I began introducing the idea of rejecting the very possibility of nuclear war because of the weapons' destructiveness. Later, as I have mentioned, I was invited to join the Emergency Committee of Atomic Scientists, of which Albert Einstein was chairman. Over the years, my wife and I supported numerous organizations whose goal was world peace.

For a while, many other scientists did the same. Then, in about 1950, the Republican senator from the state of Wisconsin, Joseph R. McCarthy, began scandalous investigations into the private lives of leading citizens suspected of communist subversion. As a consequence of the influence of what came to be known as McCarthyism, advocates of cooperation with the Soviet Union were criticized as un-American. In this environment, a number of scientists stopped making public appearances altogether. But, perhaps out of stubbornness, I refused to allow McCarthy and the anticommunists in the United States to silence me.

Ikeda: The McCarthy investigations, conducted during the Truman administration, were notorious as attacks against the freedoms of thought, speech, and political activity of anyone suspected of being a communist or a communist-sympathizer. You demonstrated admirable bravery in not allowing the climate of those times to silence you. Although from a different standpoint, I too have experienced pressures and even oppression and can understand how you felt. Your situation must have caused your wife considerable concern.

Pauling: I felt compelled to earn and keep her respect. She always understood the reasons for all my actions. And I did not want her to think I was a coward. In addition, I had my own self-respect to consider. I was determined McCarthy would not succeed in browbeating me.

My determination did not prevent our having our passports taken away. And the California Institute of Technology tried to put pressure on me. The institute's board of trustees was made up largely of conservative businessmen who disliked my being a spokesman for world peace and for cooperation with the Soviet Union. As I expressed it in my book *No More War* and in perhaps a hundred articles and papers, I was—and remain—convinced that we can make agreements with the Soviet Union to promote disarmament and that the Soviet Union will abide by them. Recent developments suggest that my conviction is well founded.

But, at the time of the McCarthy hearings, under pressure from the board of trustees to dismiss me, the president of the institute finally went so far as to relieve me of the position of chairman of the Divisions of Chemistry and Chemical Engineering, a position I had held for twenty-two years.

Although I had built the department into what it remains today— one of the greatest chemistry departments in the world—I said I had held the administrative post long enough and resigned. But professors have tenure, and merely working for peace did not constitute sufficient cause for the president to take away my professorship.

Still there were ways of putting pressure on me. Other people got raises in salary, but I did not. As a matter of fact, I took a cut when I ceased to be chairman of the division. I was told that I had to give up my laboratory space because others needed it.

When I received the Nobel Peace Prize, in 1963, the president of the institute admitted it was remarkable for one person to receive two such awards but claimed there were differences of opinion about the value of my work. I decided to leave.

I had been at the California Institute of Technology for forty-two years altogether—from the time when it was a small organization with no great reputation until it became one of the leading scientific institutions of the world. I felt I owed it a great deal but realized the time had come for me to move on.

Ikeda: The story of your struggle is encouraging. Others too were the victims of the lunacy of the McCarthy era. Egerton Herbert Norman, a Canadian diplomat, historian, and author of numerous books on Japanese topics, did a great deal to help build a democratic Japan in the postwar period. But he suffered such psychological anguish because of the McCarthy hearings that he committed suicide in Cairo, while serving as ambassador to Egypt. Norman was a cultivated man of a cheerful, sociable disposition who did not seem to be the type to take his own life. Obviously the McCarthy madness did psychological damage that is difficult for an outsider to comprehend.

Your own unwavering championing of the cause of justice has much in common with the way of life we Buddhists attempt to emulate. This way of life represents purity of determination to abide by a well-considered decision in spite of all adverse opinion and criticism. Ultimately, the United States Senate reprimanded Joseph McCarthy for his actions. The course pursued by you and your wife in the name of peace was fully vindicated.

Pauling: I have tried to encourage various groups to go ahead with their work for world peace in spite of everything. In 1957, in cooperation with Barry Commoner and Edward U. Condon, I participated in circulating a petition entitled "An Appeal by American Scientists to the Governments and Peoples of the World" to stop testing nuclear weapons. Within a short period after requests were dispatched, the signatures of 2,000 American scientists reached me in my home in Pasadena. Copies of the appeal were sent to the United Nations, to the Special Subcommittee on Radiation of the Joint Committee on Atomic Energy of the Congress of the United States, and to President Dwight D. Eisenhower. It is significant that most of the prominent geneticists, who are in the best position to know the damage radiation can do to human genes, signed the appeal.

I think my wife's work and mine can be said to have enjoyed considerable success. For instance, when she and I were in Europe, we learned that "An Appeal by American Scientists" had demonstrated to scientists in other countries that Americans are concerned about the dangers of nuclear war and of nuclear testing. The petition we submitted to the United Nations calling for a halt to testing was ultimately signed by 13,000 scientists, perhaps the largest group ever to sign such a statement.

In later years too, appeals of this kind have continued to be made, mainly by scientists. The year 1982 was especially notable in this connection. Indeed, Professor Bernard T. Feld of *The Bulletin of the Atomic Scientists* has listed twenty-five such appeals for 1982, which he has called the "year of the appeals." Three hundred people in Japan signed a petition initiated by Nobel laureate Hideki Yukawa, a signatory to the Russell-Einstein Manifesto. Scientists in the Eastern European bloc too drew up similar appeals.

Ikeda: I sympathize entirely with such movements to canvass the opinions of people at the grass-roots level. Working largely through the Soka Gakkai Youth Division, in January, 1975, we were able to present to the United Nations secretary general a petition for peace and the abolition of nuclear weapons signed by ten million people.

With the cooperation of the United Nations, we have assembled an exhibition entitled "Nuclear Weapons—a Threat to Our World," which has been presented by Soka Gakkai International in twenty-three regions in sixteen nations throughout the world and has had a tremendous impact.

Pauling: Excellent. In 1961, my wife and I continued our task by circulating among scientists and nonscientists a petition against the spread of nuclear weapons. About two hundred thousand people signed it.

Ikeda: As another instance of the scientific conscience at work, in 1957, Werner Heisenberg and a group of German scientists issued what is called the Goettingen Declaration, in which it is said that the signatories consider pure scientific research, its applications, and the instruction of youth in that field to be their proper work. They add that they willingly accept the responsibility for the results of their own activities and are therefore unwilling to remain silent on political matters. Finally they clearly state their disinclination to participate in production, experimentation, and use of nuclear weapons in any form whatsoever. Politicians must have been disturbed by such a statement from people thoroughly versed in all details of the threat nuclear weapons pose.

Pauling: Politicians occasionally react very sharply to things of that kind. The immediate official response to my peace activities was a subpoena to appear before the Subcommittee on National Security of the United States Senate. The hearing was postponed for some years.

Although I was threatened with a jail term and a fine for contempt of the Senate, the threats were not carried out. The official attitude toward me began to change when President John F. Kennedy decided that a bomb-test treaty should be concluded. From statements he made to me, I think my work played a part in causing him to reach this decision.

Ikeda: What were your associations with President Kennedy? I was invited to meet him once, but my schedule would not permit it. Later I did enjoy a friendly meeting and discussion with his brother Robert Kennedy.

Pauling: I wrote a letter to him condemning the resumption of atmospheric nuclear testing by the United States as wicked because of the effects it could have on human genetics and the likelihood of its causing cancer and the birth of deformed children. He did not answer my letter.

The only conversation I had with him occurred at a White House dinner in 1961. Mrs. Kennedy introduced me to the president, who said he hoped I would continue expressing my convictions. I was pleased to hear him say this. The government was attacking me at the time. I felt my position on nuclear tests was vindicated later when President Kennedy adopted the stand that the United States should conclude a bomb-test treaty.

Ikeda: One of the most significant examples of scientists' organizing a movement in opposition to nuclear war is the series of international meetings called the Pugwash Conferences, at which scientists from forty nations in both the East and the West have been able to meet and discuss the nuclear threat in an open way transcending ideologies. The impetus for the initiation of the Pugwash Conferences was the Einstein-Russell Manifesto of 1955. What were your relations with that declaration?

Pauling: Bertrand Russell drew up the Einstein-Russell Manifesto, of July, 1955, and Einstein signed it shortly before he died. I was not involved in composing it but was one of its eleven signers. Professor Joseph Rotblat, of the University of London, and I are the only two surviving signatories.

The manifesto pointed out the dangers of thermonuclear weapons and appealed to humanity to choose further growth, knowledge, and happiness instead of following a path leading to quarreling and death. In addition, it called for an international conference of scientists and asked that this resolution be passed

> In view of the fact that in any future world war nuclear weapons will certainly be employed and that such weapons threaten the continued existence of mankind, we urge the Governments of the world to realize, and to acknowledge publicly, that their purposes cannot be furthered by a world war, and we urge them, consequently, to find peaceful means for the settlement of all matters of dispute between them.

You are correct to say that this manifesto led to the Pugwash Conferences, initially supported by the American financier Cyrus Eaton. The first of the meetings was held in Pugwash, Nova Scotia, in July, 1957, and produced a moving and informative report on the hazards of using atomic energy for peaceful as well as belligerent ends, the problems of controlling nuclear weapons, and scientists' social responsibilities. Twenty scientists from ten nations signed the report.

Among those present at the meeting were Soviet scientists who reported to the Academy of Sciences of the U.S.S.R. and expressed their complete willingness to cooperate with scientists from other countries to ensure peace and prevent nuclear war. Their statement to this effect was signed by 198 members of the Academy of Sciences and other Soviet academies.

I attended a number of the Pugwash meetings; but after some years, the conferences departed from their original plan of discussing and attempting to prevent nuclear war. Nonetheless, they have had a significant influence in developing the present attitude that such a war between great powers must be averted at all costs.

Ikeda: Interestingly enough, it was in 1957, the year of the first Pugwash Conference, that my mentor Josei Toda, second president of Soka Gakkai, published his own declaration in the name of the prohibition of nuclear weapons. He severely censured them as a threat to the continued survival of humanity and at the same time condemned the evil inherent in the very willingness to destroy life by producing and using them. Of course, because it demands the profoundest and sincerest psychological efforts, eliminating nuclear weapons is no easy task.

Pauling: The Einstein-Russell Manifesto foresees this difficulty. I remember being especially impressed by some words in its final paragraph:

> We appeal as human beings to human beings: remember your humanity and forget the rest. If you can do so, the way lies open to a new paradise; if you cannot, there lies before you the risk of universal death.

Ikeda: The significance of this famous statement is even greater now than when the words were first written.

Pauling: I agree. I think it may have been this very statement that encouraged me to emphasize morality and ethics in *No More War*, which was first published in 1958, three years after the manifesto was issued.

Ikeda: In *No More War,* you make a statement with which I, as a Buddhist, am in complete accord:

> I believe that there is a greater power in the world than the evil power of military force, of nuclear bombs—there is the power of good, of morality, of humanitarianism. I believe in the power of the human spirit.

The issue of war and peace involves more than military preparations and political systems. It demands that we examine matters from the fundamental standpoint of the human beings responsible for both arms systems and political actions. Current notions of nuclear deterrents, primary attacks, and limited nuclear conflicts remind me of Procrustes, the bandit who tied victims to a bed and forced them to fit by stretching the small ones to the size of the frame and lopping off the heads and limbs of those who were too large. We must not condone tying billions of members of the human race to a Procrustean bed of misguided nuclear policy.

Work to Make Ourselves Happy

Pauling: I agree that fundamental human nature is the key. But, as Benjamin Franklin said when he observed improvements taking place in the physical sciences, "Oh that moral science were in as fair a way of improvement." Bertrand Russell hit on the same point when he said, "If people would only work as hard to make themselves happy as they now work to make other people unhappy, the world would be a wonderful place."

In the United States, everyone would be happier if the military budget were cut by a hundred billion dollars. The entire nation would benefit by saving this much of our wealth. But we continue spending to make unhappy the citizens of the Soviet Union, the military budget of which has consistently been a still greater burden on a nation with only a fraction of the total wealth of the United States. At one time during his presidency, Ronald Reagan, who espoused a confrontational approach and was willing to spend vast amounts of money on the military, announced that, although the Soviet Union had reached the end of its economic tether and could afford to spend no more on armaments, the United States had to keep on spending in order to stay on top.

Bertrand Russell was right. We ought to work to make ourselves happier by cutting military budgets. Of course, this might make the Russian people twice as happy as the American people.

Ikeda: I have repeatedly said that, although the consumer-oriented society and extravagant reliance on disposable goods and consequent depletion of natural resources are certainly major woes, cutting military expenses is the surest way to make maximum reduction in wasteful expenditures. As authorities in the field point out, no business could survive the kind of spendthrift luxury represented by a full-scale arms race. President Gorbachev must have seen this at an early stage in his career.

A change of approach is essential. The 1985 treaty on the elimination of intermediary-range missiles concluded between the United States and the Soviet Union shows that a small step in the right direction is possible, given the proper political determination. This reminds me of an unforgettable remark President Kennedy made in one of his speeches:

> Our problems are manmade—therefore, they can be solved by man. And man can be as big as he wants. No problem of human destiny is beyond human beings. Man's reason and spirit have often solved the seemingly unsolvable—and we believe they can do it again.
>
> —quoted from Harold Willens, *The Trimtab Factor*

Nationalism may be pinpointed as a major obstacle on the road to the creation of a new global order. Although it sometimes inspires domestic progress, in extreme, unbridled forms, patriotism can stimulate international antagonism. How would you define optimum patriotism?

Pauling: In this respect, perhaps the principles set forth in the United States Constitution and Bill of Rights—especially the Bill of Rights—should be our guides. Patriotism can work positively for progress but can also be a negative force.

In 1961, having become increasingly concerned about the spread of nuclear arms, my wife and I compiled and submitted to the United Nations "An Appeal to Stop the Spread of Nuclear Weapons." It was signed by about two hundred thousand people from forty-five countries. Later we decided to invite scientists and scholars to a conference on the same topic. The conference was held between May 2 and 7, 1961, in Oslo, Norway. Among the material on this conference published in Appendix 5 in *No More War* (anniversary edition), occurs a remarkable statement:

Restriction of loyalty to within national boundaries is obsolete and loyalty to the whole of mankind is now a necessity. Individuals must bear personal responsibility for acts contrary to the interests of mankind.

Ikeda: This is certainly true. We must become aware of ourselves as citizens of the whole world.

Pauling: This statement, issued at the end of the 1961 Oslo conference, was unanimously approved by all participants. Among its signatories were three representatives of the Soviet Union, as well as others from such nations as Poland, Czechoslovakia, and Hungary. All of them approved what amounted to a display of unbridled universal patriotism.

As an American writer has said, "Patriotism is not the last resort of the politician, it's the first resort." Some politicians appeal to the public by emphasizing support for the military. In a few instances, they may suggest eliminating certain expensive projects, like the B-2 bomber, while at the same time insisting on building up conventional military defenses.

Ikeda: In my travels around the globe, I have come to see that ordinary people can be surprisingly cosmopolitan in their views. Fear and anger, however, sometimes upset cosmopolitan equilibrium. We must be on our guard against allowing ourselves to be engulfed in emotional reactions (especially feelings of inferiority) and must strive to discern dispassionately and accurately between true pacifism and concealed belligerence. Granted the process may take time. But without doubt, educating knowledgeable and calm-thinking people to avoid obsession with the apparent advantage of the moment is the way to progress toward peace.

Pauling: We must make people constantly aware that we live on one world—the Spaceship Earth—and must consider the welfare and ecological problems of the entire planet. For instance, the United States must not ignore the harm acid rain produced by American industry does to Canadian forests. Similarly, the British must not overlook the damage acid rain from their industry does when windblown over Sweden, Norway, and Denmark.

Ikeda: Negative elements like nuclear weapons and environmental pollution—like acid rain—compel us to realize that, as you say, we live on one planet. In the economic field too, internationalization of the kind evident in multinational corporations is becoming increasingly apparent, while, unfortunately, politics, once a noble human undertaking, remains bound to national interests and therefore lags behind.

Our task is to convert such negative elements into positive elements and in this way to help people become aware of themselves as citizens of the world. This is why I have proposed that the United Nations establish "Citizens of the Earth Decade" in preparation for the twenty-first century.

Pauling: We must give primary attention to the welfare of the whole world and only secondary attention to the welfare of individual nations. Patriotism is acceptable only as long as it involves no belligerence.

Fortunately, with the exception of the Civil War, the United States has seen no military troubles among the states and has had no such trouble with Canada since 1812. We have no need to keep soldiers along the border between Canada and the United States. And, since the Mexican War (1846–1848), when the United States sent an army to Mexico to fight soldiers who wanted to overthrow a government in favor of the rich and institute one more sympathetic to the poor, we have had no trouble of that kind with Mexico. In other parts of Latin America, we have been less fortunate. Cuba is obviously a problem. United States forces occupied Nicaragua for decades. In short, we have not emulated Sweden's record of involvement in no wars since 1815.

A Remarkable Country

Ikeda: If it has not managed to stay out of wars as well as Sweden, as a melting pot of peoples of many ethnic backgrounds, the United States is especially significant in connection with cultivating citizens of the Earth. The so-called American experiment suggests many important things for the global society of the future.

Pauling: The United States is a remarkable country, attacking and solving its problems in remarkable ways. As I have said, the nation has suffered from little internal strife. Of course, we have had the difficulties of accommodating the 10 percent of the population who are Black and dealing with the problems of Hispanics. During World War II, President Roosevelt made the mistake of relying on military men, who often follow rules without thinking, and incarcerating American citizens of Japanese descent. Nonetheless, the United States remains a remarkable country.

Ikeda: The problem of the forced detention of Americans of Japanese descent during World War II was not dealt with conclusively until forty years later. Nonetheless, I see the ultimate apology issued by the United States government both as an indication that the American conscience is alive and healthy and as an element inspiring confidence in the recuperative powers of American democracy. I know many Americans of Japanese descent; and they are all, without exception, outstanding citizens of the United States.

Pauling: I might relate an interesting episode in connection with this point. Before World War II, my wife hired a Japanese gardener. When the war started, all Japanese were transported to detention camps. As a consequence, we lost our gardener. But before long, someone telephoned my wife to inform her of a young Japanese-American Nisei who, though already inducted into the American army, had two weeks' leave to settle family affairs and would like to take care of our garden during the interim. My wife and I belonged to a group that was protesting the treatment of Japanese people in California. Perhaps a member of that group suggested that my wife hire the young man.

She did hire him. But he worked only one day, because, on the night of his having been hired, a rising sun and the words, "Americans die, but Pauling loves Japs" appeared painted on our garage and mailbox.

Ikeda: I suppose this is not surprising in the light of the social conditions of the time.

Pauling: We were threatened, and the threats grew worse after word of the incident appeared in the newspapers. I had to go to Washington, D.C. on some war work; and, while I was away, the local sheriff was compelled to put a guard around our house to protect my wife. The matter got a good bit of publicity, some of it unfavorable.

Ikeda: Why were you eager to offer the young Nisei work?

Pauling: He had been born in the vicinity of Sacramento, California, and was by birth an American citizen who happened to be of Japanese descent. Because both of us were concerned to protect the rights of individual human beings, my wife, who was an officer in the Los Angeles chapter of the American Civil Liberties Union, might have hired someone who was not even an American citizen at all.

Ikeda: I am impressed by the consistency of the stand you both took. No doubt you were in sympathy with the aims of the Civil Rights movement headed by Martin Luther King, who won the Nobel Peace Prize in 1964.

I discussed matters related to the rights of minorities with Mervyn M. Dymally, Republican member of the House of Representatives and chairman of the United States Congressional Black Caucus, when I met him in 1988.

The philosophy of minority rights as expressed in Asia and Africa is crystallized in the anticolonialist spirit of the Bandung Conference of 1955 and the Five Principles of Peace. Such rights must be jealously guarded.

Pauling: In the United States, the racial-discrimination situation has improved. In 1965, my son Linus, Jr. was one of eight people who flew from Honolulu to take part in the Selma-Montgomery March led by Dr. Martin Luther King in opposition to methods used to restrict voting of Blacks in the state of Alabama. In the march, my son's group carried a banner bearing the slogan, "Hawaii knows that integration works."

Ikeda: On my numerous visits there, I have always been impressed with Hawaii as a place where several races live together in harmony.

Pauling: Linus's second wife is a Hawaiian of Japanese parentage (they were not married at the time of the Selma-Montgomery March). With a population made up of people from many different backgrounds—Hawaiian, Chinese, Japanese, Caucasian, and so on—living and working well together, Hawaii is an encouraging example to the whole world. Of course, there are other places where no racial discrimination exists.

Ikeda: In the many exchanges of opinion I have enjoyed during the past twenty years with political and cultural leaders from all over the world, the importance to global peace of summit meetings—especially between the leaders of powerful nations like the United States and the Soviet Union—has always been emphatically stated.
  In May, 1981, in Moscow, I suggested to Nikolai A. Tikhonov, then premier, that such a meeting ought to be held outside the Soviet Union, perhaps in Switzerland. Then, to my great gratification, in November, 1985, a Soviet-United States summit meeting did actually take place in Geneva. And, at that time, a treaty abolishing intermediate-range nuclear ballistic weapons was signed.
  Conditions in Eastern Europe and the Soviet Union have altered with incredible speed and dynamism since then. Still, I continue placing the greatest importance on further, person-to-person, frank, and open discussions between the leaders of these two nations.

Pauling: There can be no doubt that heart-to-heart talks between the leaders of the United States and the Soviet Union are vital to lasting world peace.

Ikeda: You have visited the Soviet Union on several occasions and are even a recipient of a Lenin Peace Award.

Pauling: Yes, I received the Lenin Peace Award in 1970 and the Lomonosov Award in 1978. Long before that, in 1958, I was made a full member of the Academy of Sciences of the Soviet Union. But perhaps you are more familiar with Soviet scientists and scholars than I am.

Ikeda: In May, 1985, when I was in Moscow—for the fourth time—to attend the opening of the exhibition entitled "Nuclear Arms— A Threat to Our World," I made a proposal concerning peace and the abolition of nuclear arms.

For the past fourteen years, Soka University has maintained direct cooperative relations with Moscow State University and has frequently conducted teacher and student exchange programs. Joint research projects between the two are beginning to bear fruit.

A dialogue between Professor A. A. Logunov, rector of Moscow State University, and myself has been published in book form under the title *The Third Rainbow Bridge*. I hope the book will transcend national boundaries and political systems and help unite peoples working for global peace in the twenty-first century.

At present, the whole world has its eyes on President Gorbachev's perestroika program of restructuring. If the tremendous economic, ethnic, and political difficulties plaguing the Soviet Union can be resolved, his program is certain to have far-reaching effects on world peace. I too am keenly interested in the democratization process generated by President Gorbachev's bold ideas. What are your views of recent developments in the Soviet Union?

Pauling: Things may be taking a turn for the better in the Soviet Union. The initial changes made by Mikhail Gorbachev constituted a great leap forward. The idea that a better international image will result from refraining from oppressing individuals with unconventional opinions seems to have taken root in the Soviet Union.

I was there last in December, 1984, to participate by invitation in the celebration of the sixtieth anniversary of the founding of the Soviet Union. I was one of an audience of three thousand in a great hall in the Kremlin. Among the members of the gathering were politicians, representatives of the seventeen Soviet republics, all of the members of the Soviet Academy of Sciences, I believe, and other distinguished guests.

I was probably invited because I am a recipient of the International Lenin Peace Award. Other recipients from other countries were present too. Although at the time I expended considerable effort trying to arrange a meeting with the late Andrei Sakharov, who was in internal exile in Gorky, I was unable to obtain permission. The president of the academy told me, "I know and you know that Sakharov doesn't have any secret information that has any value, but as long as they think he does, those people in the Kremlin are not going to let him leave."

Later, of course, Sakharov was permitted to leave Gorky and even to travel abroad and take part in political activities. This in itself was a great forward stride in Soviet policy.

In many other areas too, the Soviet Union is moving in the right direction. One example is allowing more Soviet Jews to emigrate to Israel. Certainly the Soviet Union has its problems, but Gorbachev is doing an excellent job.

Ikeda: Andrei Sakharov was called the father of the Soviet hydrogen bomb. In the West, a leading advocate of the hydrogen bomb is the Hungarian-born American physicist Edward Teller, who worked on the Manhattan Project at the outset, who is famous for his work on the hydrogen bomb, and with whom you have engaged in debate. On scientific grounds, you criticized his speaking of the "beauty" of the bomb and pointed out his errors. I have heard that, in doing this, you exerted a great influence on Andrei Sakharov.

Pauling: I did participate in a televised debate with Dr. Teller on February 22, 1958. But since that time I have refused to meet or debate with him further because I consider his debating methods improper. When speaking with me and later with the leading physicist Dr. Sidney Drell, of Stanford University, Teller claimed he could not reveal evidence verifying his statements and proving us incorrect because the material in question was classified. Dr. Drell said that Teller knew nothing that he himself did not know and that using the argument of classified material was wrong. There is no need to go into details, since Teller's debate with me has already been published in *Daedalus*, which is issued by the American Academy of Arts and Sciences, and has been rebroadcast a number of times.

In the Right Direction

Ikeda: In spite of the dramatic changes occurring in relations between the Soviet Union and the United States, many Americans seem to persist in distrusting the Soviets. What is your personal impression of the Soviet Union? The Soviet people suffered tremendously during World War II. Precisely because of the many lives lost in that conflict, today they seem to long ardently for peace.

Pauling: I agree that the Soviet people as a whole suffered greatly during World War II—as they had during the Napoleonic Wars and World War I. Although the American Civil War took a great toll, war has been less costly for the United States—about 50,000 Americans killed first in World War I and later in Korea and Vietnam. Soviet losses in World War II were very much greater than this, and there is no doubt that the Soviet people want world peace.

Ikeda: Dr. Logunov of Moscow State University told me that Soviet writers, film makers, and television directors continue today allotting a great deal of time and space to World War II so that the people will never forget the misery war inflicts.

Pauling: Distrust of the Soviet Union in the United States arises largely from powerful capitalists who fear socialism (perhaps more than communism). The United States government finds it hard to distinguish between communist and socialist regimes. For instance, they described the Sandinista Nicaraguan government as communist when it would have been better to call it socialist. And their main objection

was not so much to a socialist Nicaraguan government as to the propagation of other such governments in Central and South America.

Ikeda: The key to removing distrust is mutual understanding, for
the sake of which more extensive exchanges at all levels are essential.

Pauling: It is often said that the Soviet Union cannot be trusted
to keep treaties. In fact, however, historians who have studied this
issue agree that the record of the Soviet government in this respect is
as good as that of the United States and other countries. These specialists add that the Soviet government is actually a stickler for ob-
serving the letter of the law in treaties.

Ikeda: Fixed, even if unfounded ideas, like assumed Soviet dis-
regard for treaties can have a stupefying effect. In Japan too, the notion
of the Soviet threat has been noised abroad for decades. Familiarity
through repeated exchanges is the slow-but-sure way to eliminate such
harmful fixed ideas. Even Ronald Reagan greatly modified his formerly
vociferous doctrine of the "evil empire" after visiting Moscow.
    As far as treaties are concerned, few countries can claim to have
kept all their promises.

Pauling: The United States government has a very poor record
for keeping treaties in its dealings with the American Indians. With
respect to other treaties, its record and that of the Soviet Union are
probably on a par. Indeed, some historians praise the Soviet Union
highly on this count.

Ikeda: Shortly after Gorbachev and Reagan signed the treaty abolishing Intermediate Nuclear Forces (INFs), at the White House, in
December, 1987, I had a visit from Anatoli Adamishin, then deputy
foreign minister of the Soviet Union. During our discussion, we mentioned the summit meeting; and I called the recently concluded agreement between his nation and the United States epoch-making because
it represents the very first time a whole category of nuclear weapons
has been eliminated. Although it is true that numbers of INFs are
small in comparison with total nuclear arsenals, I nonetheless rate the
agreement very high.
    As President Kennedy implied in the passage I quoted earlier, no

matter how difficult nuclear-arms reduction may seem, human beings created those arms; and human beings can do away with them. The INF treaty proves this to be true.

Pauling: The Intermediate-Range Nuclear Forces Treaty between the Soviet Union and the United States was a good, although small, step toward the control of nuclear weapons and the goal of eliminating nuclear war from the world. My principal criticism of the treaty is that it has not and apparently will not lead to significant decreases in the armaments budgets of the two nations. The victory of the Allied Forces in the Persian Gulf war may motivate more people to support further increases in military spending, especially in high-technology systems like the Patriot. Real progress towards world peace will come only when military budgets are decreased to half their present magnitude, then again to half that, and so on until rationality is achieved.

Ikeda: No doubt economic conditions played a part in the decision to conclude the INF treaty. Since *perestroika* has done little so far to better the Soviet economy—and undeniably it faces staggering problems—reductions of the Soviet military budget and application of the funds thus freed to the needs of the people are essential.

But more important still is the growing realization of the irrationality of wasting further money on military budgets, which are themselves supremely wasteful. Perhaps a late-dawning awareness of the truth that regional wars are prodigal and bring only hardship and ruin has been influential in terminating conflicts like the Iran-Iraq war. The subsequent invasion of Kuwait by Iraqi forces and the Gulf war vividly demonstrate, however, the horrors of unrestrained militarism. In addition, it shows how imperative it is for us all to strive to make arms reduction a major trend of our times.

Pauling: Concluding treaties to decrease amounts of money spent on militarism is the best way to improve relations among national states—including of course the United States and the Soviet Union. Economic interactions proceed fairly well, and there is a good deal of trade back and forth at the present. I wish the United States and the Soviet Union would agree to support no wars in the less-developed portions of the world. Before the dramatic discrediting of communism in Eastern Europe and even in the Soviet Union in recent years, such an agreement was difficult to achieve because the United States was, and remains, in the grasp of capitalists who worry about the spread of socialism. Things may change now that formerly socialist states are enthusiastically adopting capitalist methods.

Ikeda: I had hoped that the 1989 summit meeting between presidents Bush and Gorbachev would result in a 50-percent reduction in strategic nuclear arms. Undoubtedly the two powers will reach final agreement on this point sooner or later. But, even with such a reduction, the nuclear threat will not be completely removed. Thought will have to be given immediately to the next step in the arms-reduction process.

Pauling: The next step that the United States and the Soviet Union should take is to make an agreement to cut all nuclear-weapons stockpiles in half, to stop research and development of nuclear weapons, and to ban all tests of nuclear weapons. Similar agreements—including one to prevent the spread of nuclear weapons—should be made with all other nations.

No Full-Scale Nuclear War

Ikeda: For years stubborn American adherence to the so-called Strategic Defense Initiative (SDI) program was the main stumbling block in the way of achieving final agreement on strategic nuclear-arms reductions at summit meetings. George Bush stated his intention of following the Reagan policy in this connection, but he is encountering resistance from a recalcitrant Congress. As I told Henry Kissinger not long ago, it is an error to attempt to solve the arms and security dilemma posed by nuclear weapons with just another hardline idea like SDI. Hardline approaches have obvious limitations.

Instead of relying on the development of new weapons, the United States and the Soviet Union ought to work for diplomatic efforts to inspire trust, win the support of world opinion, and contribute to the mutual prosperity of both nations.

Pauling: The danger of accidental nuclear war is increased by exploitation of space for military purposes. The Strategic Defense Initiative is, in my opinion, based on unsound scientific principles. It constitutes a serious threat to world peace and involves a great waste of money that ought to be used for the benefit of humankind.

Large segments of the population of the world lead unhappy, poverty-stricken lives. They are malnourished or starving, have wretched housing and clothing, and lack all opportunities for wholesome enjoyment. Under such circumstances, it is immoral to waste the wealth of the world on expensive military establishments.

Ikeda: A very important point. During my travels through more than forty nations, I have worked for cultural and educational exchanges and have lectured at the invitation of numerous universities. These experiences have convinced me that the best possible security system is the untiring cultivation of mutual acquaintance and respect among all peoples. Of course, consultation among political leaders is important; but, as history shows, peace achieved without understanding on all sides is always fragile.

Pauling: My many lectures and those of my wife too in all the states of the United States and in forty foreign countries have had a significant effect on the peace movement. My being a scientist has been an advantage because it has put me in a position to know about nuclear physics, chemistry, biology, and medicine. Dr. Teller and others cannot honestly claim that I lack facts and do not understand the problems under debate. Furthermore, general respect for science inspires people to pay attention when scientists advance strong opinions.

Ikeda: Yes, people find what scientists have to say convincing. What points have you emphasized in your recent speeches?

Pauling: Not long ago, in Yugoslavia, I gave a public lecture about vitamins and health and a short statement on world peace. I also participated in writing a declaration by scientists on world peace and other problems. In recent talks, I have stressed the idea that the existence of nuclear weapons makes it impossible for the United States and the Soviet Union to go to war deliberately; that is, unless an accident prompts belligerence from one side or the other. As long as leaders remain rational and their political systems continue to function, we will have no full-scale nuclear war. Since this is true, why spend vast sums on such arms?

The test of the strength of agreements among nations in the future will depend on how successful all can be in reducing military budgets. We must therefore strive to work for such reductions. This has been the aspect of the issue that I have stressed in recent lectures.

Ikeda: I have always stressed the importance of the United Nations as the central organ for world peace. In a proposal for global peace made at the beginning of 1989, I said that, given the current international multipolarity, making the United Nations the heart of all efforts to create a new political and economic order is the most practical approach.

The United Nations played an unusually vigorous role in the early developments leading to the Gulf War. Unfortunately, Secretary General Perez de Cuellar was unable to reach an understanding with Saddam Hussein; and the reins of control slipped from his hands and into those of President Bush. Since the end of the war, much has been said of a New World Order. But so far, the process has produced only meager results. Surely allowing the United Nations to take the lead in the undertaking would be the best way.

I have already proposed establishing a United Nations Conflict-Prevention Center for the sake of averting crises like the one in the Persian Gulf. Further, as part of the activities of nongovernmental organizations (NGOs) in support of the United Nations, I have proposed an exhibition entitled "War and Peace" and a Peace Summit of NGOs.

Pauling: I agree that we must support the United Nations, UNESCO, and the United Nations Peace-Keeping Forces. Generally speaking, I oppose awarding the Nobel Peace Prize to organizations because I believe that Alfred Nobel, the founder of the prizes, had in mind individuals who make great contributions to world peace. Nonetheless, it was an excellent thing to give it to the United Nations Forces in 1988.

I support the United Nations as an important international organization in the struggle to achieve and maintain world peace.

You mention your own proposal for a crisis-prevention center. Thirty years ago, I advanced an appeal for a large-scale research center for world peace. Since then, much progress has been made, although the great international research center I looked forward to has not been forthcoming. There are, however, many national and private research centers for world peace; and they make important contributions.

In February, 1982, thirty-three scientists from twenty-two nations took part in a symposium on "Scientists, the Arms Race, and Disarmament." The meeting was held in Ajaccio [Corsica] France and was jointly organized by UNESCO and the Pugwash Conferences on Science and World Affairs. The final statement of the meeting says that the important work of providing information for people concerned with implementation of disarmament measures can no longer be left to a small number of scientists. It should be the duty of all scientists to study these matters. The Ajaccio statement ends in the following way:

> The continuing arms race with no prospect for its reversal in sight, and the ensuing threat of a nuclear holocaust, produce fear, frustration, and a feeling of helplessness and hopelessness among people, particularly in the young generation. They also lead to apathy and pessimism in the ranks of the scientific community. But a formulation of specific tasks may hearten and activate scientists to do something worthwhile and enable them to return science back to its true calling.

We believe that the above recommendation, including those addressed to the United Nations and UNESCO, if implemented, would provide the much needed optimism that it is still possible to prevent catastrophe; and the hope—indeed the conviction—that scientists have an important role to play in the creation of conditions for a secure and peaceful world.

Chernobyl

Ikeda: Much discussion has been made of supervision of nuclear energy since the accident that occurred at the Chernobyl nuclear plant. Some have argued that estimates of the damage done were extravagant. Others disagree. Be that as it may, nuclear energy ought to be controlled for the safety of everyone. It seems to me that the first step toward the abolition of both nuclear and conventional armament should be direct control of nuclear energy by the United Nations. What are your thoughts on international supervision of nuclear energy?

Pauling: I am opposed to nuclear power plants for several reasons. First, usually, the destruction of the element uranium in these plants is treated lightly. It is wrong to destroy an element merely to generate extra energy for human beings living now. In a thousand or ten thousand years, the world may require uranium for a purpose about which we are currently ignorant. Another problem with nuclear plants is dealing with the wastes they generate. Still another is illustrated by the Chernobyl disaster. I agree with you that international supervision of nuclear energy is a good idea.

Ikeda: Of course, the true core issue is the development of an alternative source of energy, one that is satisfactory and safe in the long view. Diverse conditions prevailing throughout the world make it hard to select energy sources of universal applicability. Nonetheless, the issue must be addressed; and part of the solution must be revising the nature of a civilization that squanders too much of everything, including energy.

Pauling: More money should be spent on research on solar power as a substitute for nuclear energy. Solar power is most desirable because it entails no alteration of the Earth's surface temperatures. Sunlight, which naturally warms the Earth, can be converted into electricity; and, in the course of time, the electricity is degraded to thermal energy. We are not spending enough money on the technological problems connected with this very good source of energy. In addition, solar energy is renewable and can be used indefinitely. In relying on coal, oil, and nuclear power we are exhausting one or another of the Earth's resources.

Reactions throughout the world at present are various on the question of energy sources. Many nations are beginning to rely on nuclear power and are investing heavily in new plants. In the United States, on the other hand, great opposition has forced several completed or partially completed nuclear plants out of commission. And, as soon as we can do so economically, we must put the remaining nuclear plants out of commission too. Then we should rely on other sources: geothermal energy and especially solar energy. Japan, like California, is well situated to make use of geothermal sources. Tidal energy and wind energy too are promising possibilities.

Secretary for Peace

Ikeda: For a long time, you have advocated a world law for the sake of global peace. In connection with this, do you think a world federation will someday unify all the peoples of the globe?

Pauling: World law should be accepted by all nations. The World Court could serve in a far more effective way if, in cases of infraction, appearance before it were compulsory. No nation should be allowed to refuse to appear, as the United States has done on several occasions.

I do not believe there should be an all-powerful world government. There is safety in having a large number of essentially autonomous nations. At the present, the human race is very heterogeneous. Such heterogeneity enhances the richness of life and should be preserved to the maximum extent.

Ikeda: I agree. The problem, however, remains the sovereign rights of national states. In the past, states have considered it their privilege to resort to armed conflict in order to protect their interests. But, as the scale and destructiveness of war grew at an accelerated pace, it became necessary to impose limits on the unconditional exercise of states' rights. As you have pointed out, the emergence of nuclear weapons has made all-out warfare an impossibility. Now that their unbridled use can lead to the annihilation of humanity, we are compelled to deemphasize state interests and sovereign rights and afford primary concern to the interests and rights of the human race.

Recently a certain American intellectual, who has been good enough to take notice of my several proposals for peace, wrote me to suggest replacing ministries of army, navy, and defense with ministries of peace. I think this is an excellent idea and enthusiastically advanced it in the proposal I submitted to the United Nations Conference on Arms Reduction. Special consideration should be paid to this proposal by Japan, with its peace-oriented constitution; Costa Rica, which has totally abolished its military establishment; South Pacific nations that have joined in an antinuclear pact; and the North European nations that are supporters of arms reduction.

Pauling: The idea of a ministry of peace is fine. It corresponds to my own notion of a secretary for peace in the United States Cabinet. We need someone whose job is to advise presidents and top leaders about nonmilitary ways of preserving peace in the world. This is why I am very pleased to be collaborating with you in this present dialogue.

The minister, or secretary, for peace should study the suggestions made by Philip Morrison and his associates about ten years ago in his book *The Price of Defense*. Morrison's group, called the Boston Group, analyzed the United States military budget and concluded that, at the time, it could be reduced from 225 to 150 billion dollars—a reduction of 75 billion—with an actual increase in national security. They pointed to billions of dollars wasted on developing weapons systems that are never to be of any value. For instance, the B-2 bomber encountered many serious problems requiring vast sums to rectify. Why throw away such amounts on an airplane that thoughtful analysts consider a waste of money to begin with?

Ikeda: That is a very significant, concrete example of the kind of thing all nations must scrupulously guard against.

Pauling: Yes. In addition to maintaining that we could save 75 billion dollars on the budget, the Boston Group argued—and supported their argument—that such a reduction would cause no increase in unemployment since military expenditures are labor-poor. In other words, they do not generate good salaries as do such labor-rich activities as the production of civilian goods. The 75 billion saved on military expenditures could be used to create new jobs, thus averting the danger of increased unemployment. Studies of this kind ought to be followed up, and such would be part of the task of the secretary for peace.

Ikeda: Work of this kind could help the secretary for peace devise ways to alter the traditional historical current whereby technological innovation has often been associated with the production of ever larger, more murderous, and more destructive weapons.

Pauling: As you say, innovation has usually been associated with militarism, a field in which the United States has often taken the lead. We developed the atomic bomb in 1945, four years ahead of the Soviet Union. In 1960, we started adding multiple, independently directable, reentry vehicles to our big rockets. The Soviet Union undertook a similar task in 1965 but still has not finished the job. They still have larger warheads than the United States, which is ahead in directing smaller warheads to their targets more accurately. Since the United States' gross national product is twice as big as that of the Soviet Union, the fraction of that product the Soviets must devote to the military budget is twice the corresponding fraction the Americans must spend on the same kind of thing. This plus a steadily weakening economy means that the Soviet Union is even more eager than the United States to trim its military expenses.

Unfortunately, wars persist, sometimes with the active fostering of the United States or the Soviet Union. It is essential that all the developed nations adopt a policy of never selling or giving weapons to smaller nations and of supporting no wars. They must cooperate in efforts to solve long-standing disputes and improve the lots of peoples all over the world by encouraging the development of a stable society. The prevention of nuclear war and the elimination of war in general constitute the most important of all problems. I believe that every person, every group, every city, and every country should work on this problem in all available ways.

Ikeda: Yes, precedence must be given first to refraining from the use of nuclear weapons and then to their total elimination with the greatest possible speed.

Actually, however, the possibility of a nuclear war seems remote. And this makes essential the fast reduction of conventional weapons. The Gulf War showed how important technology is in modern combat. Rapid technological progress intensifies weapons' destructiveness, thus making effort in the direction of disarmament all the more vital.

The Immorality of War

Pauling: Nuclear war is the ultimate immorality. But the immorality of war is not limited to the use of nuclear weapons. As early as biblical times, noncombatants were killed off in warfare. After the walls of Jericho fell, for example, the Israelites slaughtered all the women and children in the city.

In later times, however, combat came to be generally limited to soldiers—mostly young men—although kings too were sometimes killed in battle. Even when nations were at war, women and children were generally safe. In the American Civil War, for instance, casualties were mostly soldiers. Some bombings occurred during World War I; but, in World War II, both the British and the Americans adopted a policy of bombing cities—for example, Amsterdam, Hamburg, and Dresden—thus destroying thousands of civilians. Such acts are highly immoral. It is shocking that the modern world still does not ban war as totally degenerate. In our age, not even victors benefit from war. This aspect of the struggle for peace deserves special emphasis.

Ikeda: I agree entirely. As weapons have grown more destructive and national states more confident of their sovereign rights, large-scale, indiscriminate slaughter has become a commonplace of war. A backward look at the development of modern warfare makes apparent the extent to which human beings have become subservient to the weapons they have created. To alter this situation, each individual must strive to attain wisdom and enlightenment. We must do all we can to hasten the arrival of the day when the enlightened commonality of the human race assumes the lead in the work of preserving peace. In this connection, your quotation in *No More War*, from the words of your good friend Professor George B. Kistiakowsky is highly pertinent:

> There simply is not enough time left before the world explodes. Concentrate . . . on organizing, with so many others who are of like mind, a mass movement for peace such as there has not been before.

Pauling: If they are not misled by false statements from politicians and authorities, the people will recognize the need for world peace and their own responsibilities in achieving it. The power of the people to set politicians on the right track has been demonstrated a number of times during recent decades. I believe that, in the near future, a mass movement for peace, as described by Dr. Kistiakowsky, will lead to very significant progress.

Ikeda: Often presented as ideal statesmen, the ancient Indian kings Ashoka (died 232 B.C.) and Kanishka (possibly the first half of the second century) were both devout Buddhists. Their approach to governing was imbued with the spirit of Buddhist compassion. Virtual embodiments of this philosophy, the flourishing Buddhist cultures they built in their peaceful nations are outstanding in all human history.

Although wars among believers in different religions have undeniably taken high tolls in human lives, numerous religions have exerted themselves unstintingly in the name of world peace. What is your opinion of peace movements conducted by people of religious faith?

Pauling: As you say, religious wars in the past have taken great tolls in human life. Indeed, as events in India, the Middle East, and other regions show, they continue to do so. Although the struggle between rich, property-holding Protestants and poor, laboring Catholics in Northern Ireland has a primarily economic basis, religion too plays a part in it. Of course, Catholics and Protestants have fought for centuries in the British Isles and elsewhere.

A few religions have worked for world peace on the basis of absolute pacifism. But, even in the United States, the Protestants began to take a moderately active interest in such work only in the last decade or two.

As to my own evaluation of peace movements based on religion, in general, I think they are fine. But problems sometimes arise. For example, the American Quakers are active in the work for world peace but refuse to participate in meetings attended by communists. For this reason, they broke up a meeting the British convened at Oxford because representatives from the Soviet Union had been invited. My wife and I, who were attending the meeting, could not understand their attitude. We work with all peace organizations because we need them. But not all religious groups see eye to eye with this attitude.

Ikeda: Undeniably much human blood has been shed in the name of religion; and, sadly, some of the wounds caused by religious conflicts remain unhealed. A religion that fails to contribute to human happiness and peace is useless, worse, it is pernicious. This is why I have long insisted that, in considering their roles in society it is essential to divide religions into two groups: those that work for the sake of vested authority and those that work for the good of humanity in general.

The pattern prevailing in many religions is one in which human beings are subjected to the rule of a god or some other absolute authority. Under such circumstances, human beings become means in the name of religious authority; and their very lives are sometimes sacrificed. I witnessed something of the fearsome aspects religion can assume when I examined mounds of human remains at a site once occupied by offices of the Inquisition in Lima, Peru. Any religion that sacrifices human life in the name of its own authority is wicked.

Religions ought to recognize the good of humanity as both the source of their being and the goal of their actions. The sole valid reason for a religion to exist is to contribute to the well-being and peace of the human race. The religion to which my fellow believers and I devote ourselves exists solely for the sake of humanity.

The members of Soka Gakkai International are all good citizens of the one hundred and fifty nations in which they live. All of them work steadily and unflaggingly in the name of peace. Their goals are the happiness of humanity, the prosperity of the whole world, and the rejection of war and all forms of violence. For this reason, we are especially eager to do everything we can to eliminate nuclear arms.

The Dilemma
of the Absolute Pacifist

Pauling: I certainly would support a Buddhist drive for peace; but, as I have said, I support all peace movements, even those conducted by communists. But I have doubts about absolute pacifism. What are absolute pacifists to do in a world that is not populated by absolute pacifists? Would it be possible to pursue an absolutely pacifist course under another Adolph Hitler, who wanted to dominate the world and eliminate everyone except German Aryans?

During World War II, some of my students were pacifists. One of them, an idealist, a Jew, and a vegetarian, was imprisoned. Since the prison authorities refused to recognize his vegetarianism and insisted on serving him meat, he nearly starved. Once released from jail, he was almost imprisoned a second time for failing to register for the draft. At his second trial, the judge asked whether he believed in God. Although he may well have believed in God, he confused the issue by arguing with the judge over the definition of the term. Still, on this occasion, he managed to stay out of jail.

With the exception of cases like his, the United States authorities were lenient with conscientious objectors and allowed them to work off their military obligations at various tasks. One of my students worked in a California lumber camp with other conscientious objectors. Two or three others worked with me on war projects, but I had to convince them that our tasks were too remote from fighting the enemy to trouble their consciences.

A German friend, a gifted violinist, physicist, and mathematician, was a pacifist who nonetheless was at first inducted into the German army. For a while, he operated an antiaircraft battery—he wrote me saying he thanked God he never hit anything—but later was taken out of the army and assigned to a factory where he applied his knowledge of mechanical processes in improving operational efficiency.

In spite of his brilliance, he was not made a professor until he was sixty years old because the Nazis would not award professorship to anyone who was not a member of their party. Consequently, he had a hard time making a living. Nonetheless, unlike many much less fortunate individuals, he survived the war.

Ikeda: The problem of absolute pacifism is and always has been difficult. In both theory and practice, it is hard to draw a line clearly dividing right from wrong in connection with it. Although understandably a thoroughly confirmed, absolute pacifist might be willing to face death for his faith, the political efficacy of absolute pacifism is sometimes problematic. As you say, what good would an absolute pacifist be able to do under a Hitler-like regime?

We have already mentioned Einstein's predicament in feeling impelled by the Nazi threat to recommend to President Roosevelt that the United States go ahead with research leading to the production of the atomic bomb. He was a pacifist in a world not inhabited completely by fellow pacifists:

> I was well aware of the dreadful danger which would threaten mankind were the experiments to prove successful. Yet I felt impelled to take the step because it seemed probable that the Germans might be working on the same problem with every prospect of success. I saw no alternative but to act as I did, although I have always been a convinced pacifist.

> —*Einstein on Peace*

He was afraid of what might happen if the Nazis succeeded in the nuclear research he knew they were conducting at the time. He called himself a convinced, not an absolute, pacifist. Nonetheless, the following quotation from an apologia he published in Japanese newspapers after World War II suggests that absolute pacifism was his ideal.

> Gandhi, the greatest political genius of our time, indicated the path to be taken. He gave proof of what sacrifice man is capable once he has discovered the right path. His work on behalf of India's liberation is living testimony to the fact that man's will, sustained by an indomitable conviction, is more powerful than material forces that seem insurmountable.

> —*Einstein on Peace*

In the past, international relations have generally been controlled exclusively by diplomats and politicians. Today, however, sophisticated developments in technology and transportation have greatly altered the traditional arrangement. On one level, it has become more common for supreme leaders of national states to meet person to person. On another level, tourism and cultural and sports events greatly accelerate the pace at which ordinary peoples come to know and understand each other, thus putting a more generally human face on the way history is made. This is as it must be. Instead of allowing themselves to be led about by the noses at the beck and call of national states, the ordinary citizens must assume the principal role in history.

Before concluding our dialogue, I should like to touch briefly on Japan's role in the contemporary world. Although the Japanese people themselves may not always·enjoy the fruits of national affluence as fully as they would like, Japan has become a great economic power and as such is expected by other nations to make suitable contributions to the management of the world. As the only nation ever to have suffered an atomic bombing, Japan certainly has a mission of contributing to the peace of the whole planet. Since you have visited Japan often and understand our nation well, your advice in this connection would be most welcome.

Pauling: Japan must continue refusing to rely on a large military force and refraining from developing nuclear weapons. In this way, Japan can be a leader in the drive for world peace. As a consequence of her rapid technological growth, Japan has become one of the most important nations. The health of the Japanese people has improved greatly in the last fifty years. For example, life expectancy has become much higher than it was in the Japan of the 1930s.

Japan has made a step in the direction of freeing the world of war by limiting its military establishment since the end of World War II. I realize that steps are being taken toward expanding the armed forces. But part of the prosperity of the nation in the past twenty-five years has been made possible by the absence of a great military drain (of the usual 10 or 20 percent of the gross national product) on the budget. I can see no reason for Japan to assume the burden of a large military force.

Glossary

Absolute pacifism   The belief that waging war by a state and the participation in war and the use of violence by an individual are absolutely wrong, under any circumstances, including self-defense.

Ascorbic Acid   See *Vitamin C.*

Astronomy   The branch of science that studies the motion and the nature of the planets, stars, and galaxies. More generally, the study of matter and energy in the universe. Astronomy is considered to be the oldest of the pure sciences.

Beriberi   A disease that results from a deficiency of vitamin B_1 (thiamine), characterized by loss of appetite and weight, disturbed nerve functions, fluid retention, and heart failure. The disease is common in parts of Asia where the diet is limited to highly milled rice, but it is rare in the United States.

Biotin   A B-complex vitamin that aids in body growth. It is found in liver, egg yolk, and yeast. Biotin was once known as vitamin H.

Bodhisattva   See *Buddhism.*

Brain death   Irreversible unconsciousness with total loss of brain function, usually determined by loss of reflex activity and respiration and fixed, dilated pupils, although the heart continues to beat. Legal definitions of brain death vary from country to country and, within the United States, from state to state. In general, electrical activity of the brain must be totally absent on at least two electroencephalograms taken 12 to 14 hours apart.

Buddhism   A religion and philosophy founded in India in the 6th and

101

5th centuries B.C. by Siddhartha Gautama, who is called the Buddha. Buddhism teaches the practice of meditation and the observance of moral precepts. Reality is defined in terms of cause and effect; reincarnation is among the accepted doctrines. The central concept of **Mahayana** (Great Vehicle) **Buddhism** is that all beings have the innate potential of achieving Buddhahood. Its ideal, for both layman and monk, is the *bodhisattva*—one who achieves perfection, but delays entry into nirvana (state of supreme bliss) until all others have been enlightened.

Buddhism spread to Ceylon (3rd century A.D.) and Tibet (7th century A.D.). It entered China in the 1st century A.D., spreading to Korea and Japan in the 4th and 6th centuries, respectively. Still flourishing in Asia, Buddhism has some influence in the West.

Carbon   A nonmetallic element present in virtually all living organisms and organic matter.

Chemical bond   Bonding that accounts for the grouping of atoms into molecules, ions, crystals, and compounds.

Coleoptera   The order of beetles and weevils with front wings converted to sheaths for hind wings.

Cosmology   The branch of science that aims at a comprehensive theory of the creation, evolution, and structure of the entire universe.

Diabetes mellitus   A chronic disorder of metabolism due to partial or total lack of insulin secretion by the pancreas or to the inability of *insulin* to function normally in the body. Symptoms include excessive thirst and urination, weight loss, and the presence of excessive amounts of sugar in the blood and urine.

DNA (Deoxyribonucleic acid)   A large molecule shaped like a double spiral and found primarily in the nucleus of the cell. DNA contains the cells' genetic information, which is coded in the sequence of subunits.

Electron   A negatively charged atomic particle that surrounds and orbits the *nucleus,* creating a cloud or charge. Electrons in the outermost orbit determine an atom's electrical and chemical properties.

Entomology   The study of insects, which comprise about 675,000 species—about nine-tenths of all classified animal species.

Euthanasia   The deliberate act of causing another's death to relieve pain and suffering. Euthanasia may be active—by the use of artificial means, such as drugs—or passive—by withholding treatment or medication necessary to prolong life. Also called mercy killing.

Genetic engineering   The process of controlling or altering the genetic makeup of an organism by manipulating and recombining the genetic material (DNA).

Glucose   A simple sugar that is the major source of energy for the body. Glucose is eaten in certain foods, especially fruits, and is produced by the breakdown of other carbohydrates. Glucose is absorbed into the blood from the intestines; excess amounts are stored in the liver.

Gross National Product (GNP)   A nation's total output in goods and services for a given period of time, usually one year. The three major components of GNP are consumer purchases, private investment, and government spending. Usually reported quarterly, GNP is closely watched as an indicator of a nation's economy.

Hectare   In the metric system of measurement, an area of land equivalent to 10,000 square meters or 2.47 acres.

Hemoglobin   Found in red blood cells, hemoglobin is the complex compound that contains the non-protein, iron-rich pigment *heme* and the protein *globin*.

Hepatitis   Inflammation of the liver, characterized by jaundice (yellowing of the skin and the whites of the eyes, caused by the accumulation of bile pigment in the blood), loss of appetite, discomfort, enlarged and abnormally functioning liver, and dark urine. The inflammation may be caused by bacterial or viral infection, infestation with parasites, alcohol, drugs, or transfusion of incompatible blood. Hepatitis can be mild or severe, even life-threatening.

Humanism   A philosophical and literary movement in which human values and capabilities are the central focus. The term and the point of view were originally associated with the Italian Renaissance. In general, humanism denotes an emphasis on lasting human values, respect for science, and study of the classics.

Hybrid atomic orbitals   In chemical bonding, the complex process of forming bonds by blending orbitals.

Immunology   The study of the body's response to invasion by such substances as bacteria, viruses, fungus, and transplanted tissue.

Insulin   A hormone secreted by the pancreas that regulates the metabolism of *glucose* (sugar), carbohydrates, and fats. Inadequate levels of insulin lead to metabolic disorders and excessive levels of glucose associated with *diabetes mellitus.* Insulin is also the name of the drug made from natural hormones or synthetic materials and used to treat diabetes mellitus.

Jericho   An ancient city in Palestine, in the Jordan valley, north of the Dead Sea. According to the Bible, Joshua took Jericho from the Canaanites by having his army surround the city and shouting so loudly that the walls collapsed.

Lepton   One of the elementary subparticles that is believed to constitute the fundamental building blocks of all matter. See *meson, quark, quark theory.*

Macromolecule   A molecule that contains a very large number of atoms, usually built from repeating groups of smaller molecules.

Mahayana Buddhism   See *Buddhism.*

Megavitamin therapy   Therapy based on the theory that the intake of very large doses of vitamins will prevent and cure many physical and psychological disorders.

Meson   A subatomic, unstable particle that is intermediate in mass between a *proton* and an *electron.* Mesons are found in cosmic rays and in the nuclei of atoms.

Molecular biology   The branch of biology that is concerned with studying chemical structures and processes of biological phenomena at the molecular level. Molecular biology is particularly concerned with the study of proteins, nucleic acids, enzymes (the macromolecules essential to life processes), the molecular basis of inheritance, and protein synthesis.

Molecule   The smallest particle of a compound that has all the properties of that compound. Molecules are comprised of two or more atoms, either of the same element or of two or more different elements. For example, H_2O is a molecule of water; it is made up of two atoms of hydrogen and one of oxygen.

Mutation   A change in genetic structure that may occur spontaneously or may be caused by radiation, chemicals, or genetic engineering. Such a change results in a new, inheritable characteristic. Mutation is important in the process of evolution.

Newton's Universal Law of Gravitation   Isaac Newton was the first to recognize that the force holding any object to the earth is the same as the force that holds the moon and the plants in their orbits. Because this force acts throughout the universe, it is often called universal gravitation.

According to Newton's law, the force between any two bodies is directly proportional to the product of their masses and inversely proportional to the square of the distance between them.

Niacin   A B-complex vitamin necessary for the normal functioning of the nervous system and the gastrointestinal tract. Sources rich in niacin are meats, fish, eggs, nuts, and wheat germ. Severe niacin deficiency causes *pellagra.*

Nisei   Japanese for "second born," the term refers to second generation Japanese in the United States.

During World War II, all persons of Japanese ancestry living on the West Coast of the United States were forced from their homes and placed in detention centers. It was not until the last few years that the United States government formally apologized for the detentions and granted compensation.

Nuclear fission The process by which a *nucleus* absorbs a neutron, becomes unstable, and splits into two nearly equal nuclei. Fission energy is obtained by bombarding uraniun-235 with slow neutrons in order to split it. The reaction releases an average of 2.5 neutrons, and a chain reaction is possible provided that at least one neutron per fission is captured by another nucleus and produces another fission.

In the atomic bomb, the number of neutrons that produce additional fission is greater than one and the reaction increases rapidly to an explosion. In a nuclear reactor, where the chain reaction is controlled, the number of neutrons captured and nuclei split must be exactly one to maintain a steady reaction rate.

Nuclear fission was discovered in 1938 by Otto Hahn and Fritz Strassman. Lise Meitner and Otto Frisch explained the process in 1939.

Nuclear fusion The process by which two nuclei combine to form a single heavier *nucleus.* Temperatures greater than 1,000,000°C are necessary to initiate a fusion or thermonuclear reaction. Some scientists believe that once practical, controlled fusion is achieved, it will have great advantages over nuclear fission as an alternative source of energy.

Nucleus The central core of an atom, the nucleus consists of positively charged particles (protons) and uncharged particles (neutrons).

Orthomolecular medicine The theory and practice of medicine according to which physical disease and mental illness can be cured by restoring the optimum amounts of substances (such as vitamins) normally present in the body.

Pacifism Opposition to violence, especially war, through individual or collective action. Pacifism is often connected with international movements that have disarmament as a goal. See *absolute pacifism.*

Pellagra A disease caused by the deficiency of *niacin* in the diet. It is characterized by inflammation of the skin and tongue, diarrhea, and various emotional and mental symptoms.

Perestroika Russian for "restructuring," *perestroika* is the name for Soviet President Mikhail Gorbachev's sweeping campaign for restructuring the Soviet system. The program had three main areas of concentration: *glasnost*—more openness and access to public information; democratization—greater civic involvement in the political process; and restructuring the centrally planned, heavily bureaucratized state economy.

Photoelectric effect The emission of electrons by certain substances, especially metals, when light falls on their surfaces. The effect was discovered by Heinrich Hertz in 1887 and explained by Albert Einstein in 1905.

Photon A minute packet of energy of electromagnetic radiation. Einstein originated the concept in 1905 in his explanation of the photoelectric effect in which he proposed that discrete energy packets exist in the transmission of light. All photons travel at the speed of light. Photons are considered to be among the subatomic particles.

Physical chemistry The branch of science that combines the principles and methods of physics and chemistry. Physical chemistry includes such important topics as chemical equilibrium, electro-chemistry, molecular structure, molecular weight, reaction rate, and states of matter.

Psychosomatic Refers to the interaction of the mind and the body, especially how emotional conflicts affect physical symptoms. A psychosomatic sickness is an emotional disturbance that manifests itself as a physical disorder such as childhood asthma, ulcers, hypertension, and possibly heart disease.

Quantum Theory The modern physical theory which states that energy and some other physical properties exist in tiny, discrete amounts. Older theories of classical physics held that these properties could vary continuously. The theory of relativity and quantum theory form the theoretical basis of modern physics.

Quark   Any of a group of hypothetical subparticles thought to be the basic components of matter. Just as protons and neutrons make up atomic nuclei, these particles themselves are thought to consist of quarks. Physicists have attempted to observe a quark in a free state, but have never been able to do so.

Quark theory   The theory which states that matter is composed of subatomic particles—*quarks, leptons,* and *mesons.*

Reincarnation   The religious and philosophical belief that the soul is reborn into successive existences, which may be human, animal, or even vegetable. Belief in reincarnation is most characteristic of several Asian religions, including *Buddhism.*

Relativity   The physical theory, formulated by Albert Einstein, that discarded the concept of absolute motion and instead recognizes only relative motion between two systems or frames of reference. Space and time are no longer viewed as separate and independent entities, but rather as space-time—a four-dimensional continuum.
   In 1905, Einstein formulated the *Special Theory of Relativity* which states that the laws of nature are the same in different moving systems and also apply to the propagation of light, so that the measured speed of light is constant for all observers regardless of the observer or of the source of light. From these hypotheses, Einstein reformulated the mathematical equations of physics. In 1915, he expanded the special theory into the *General Theory of Relativity* that is mainly concerned with large-scale effects of gravitation.

Rickets   A condition found primarily in children, caused by vitamin D deficiency. It is characterized by bone abnormalities. Prevention and treatment include among other things a diet adequate in vitamin D and exposure to sunlight.

Schizophrenia   A mental disorder characterized by extreme distortions of reality, withdrawal from social contacts, and disturbances of thought, language, perception, and emotional response.

Scurvy   A condition caused by lack of *vitamin C* in the diet. It is characterized by anemia, weakness, and bleeding gums.

Sickle-cell anemia A hereditary blood disorder that occurs almost exclusively among blacks and some peoples from the Mediterranean basin, in which the red blood cells assume distorted, sickle-like shapes. Due to a genetically transmitted chemical abnormality, the red blood cells are fragile and subject to rupture, which causes chronic anemia. There is no cure for the disorder, and many sufferers die young.

Soka Gakkai Soka Gakkai today can most correctly be described as an international lay Buddhist society, founded in Japan in 1930 by Japanese educator Tsunesaburo Makiguchi, and composed of adherents to the teachings of Nichiren Daishonin (1222–1282). Based on the Buddhist philosophy of absolute respect for the dignity of life, activities of the organization promote peace, culture, and education. Soka Gakkai has been named an NGO member of the United Nations, especially concerned with the problems of refugees and the environment. It is the parent organization of the Min-On Concert Association, Japan's largest subscription concert association, promoting cultural exchange through the international language of music and other cultural organizations like Tokyo Fuji and Fuji Art Museums, and the Institute of Oriental Philosophy. Third president Daisaku Ikeda founded Soka University and affiliated elementary and secondary schools and kindergartens. Soka Gakkai is now headed by fifth president Einosuke Akiya, and president of Soka Gakkai International is Daisaku Ikeda. There are more than eight million members registered in 115 countries. (The Komei party, although founded by Soka Gakkai, has been an independent political party since 1970.)

Toxicity The extent to which something is poisonous.

Universalism A religious doctrine which states that it is God's purpose to save every individual from sin through divine grace.

Vitamin An organic compound required in the diet of humans for normal growth and maintenance of life. Vitamins are the only source of certain coenzymes that are necessary for metabolism—the biochemical processes that support life. Classified alphabetically, vitamins are either fat-soluble or water-soluble. Vitamins A, D, E, and K are fat-soluble, which means that they can accumulate and be stored in body fat. B-complex vitamins and vitamin C are water-soluble and they are rapidly excreted in urine. Inadequate intake of vitamins can cause deficiency diseases.

Vitamin C   The water-soluble vitamin contained in citrus fruits, tomatoes, peppers, cabbage, potatoes, and berries. Although most animals can synthesize vitamin C, it is necessary in the diet of humans to prevent scurvy. Vitamin C is rapidly excreted in urine, so relatively large amounts are required. The vitamin is necessary for a variety of metabolic functions and the formation of collagen (a protein important in the formation of connective tissue).

Index